Nature and Causes of Homosexuality: A Philosophic and Scientific Inquiry

This volume is published in hardback as Volume 3 of the monograph series *Research on Homosexuality*.

Series Editor: John P. De Cecco, PhD, Director, Center for Research and Education in Sexuality, San Francisco State University, and editor, *Journal of Homosexuality*.

Volumes in this series include:

Homosexuality and the Law
(The hardbound edition of Volume 5, Nos. 1/2 of the *Journal of Homosexuality*. Guest Editor: Donald C. Knutson, JD). Fall/Winter 1979/80.

Historical Perspectives on Homosexuality
(The hardbound edition of Volume 6, Nos. 1/2 of the *Journal of Homosexuality*. Guest Editors: Sal Licata, PhD and Robert Petersen, PhD Candidate). Fall/Winter 1980/81.

Nature and Causes of Homosexuality: A Philosophic and Scientific Inquiry
(The hardbound edition of Volume 6, No. 4 of the *Journal of Homosexuality*. Guest Editor: Noretta Koertge, PhD). Summer 1981.

Homosexuality and Psychotherapy
(The hardbound edition of Volume 7, Nos. 2/3 of the *Journal of Homosexuality*. Guest Editor: John Gonsiorek, PhD). Winter/Spring 1981/82

Alcoholism and Homosexuality
(The hardbound edition of Volume 7, No. 4 of the *Journal of Homosexuality*. Guest Editors: Thomas O. Ziebold, PhD and John Mongeon). Summer 1982.

Homosexuality in Literature
(The hardbound edition of Volume 8, Nos. 3/4 of the *Journal of Homosexuality*.
Guest Editor: Stuart Kellogg). Spring/Summer 1983.

This series is published by The Haworth Press, Inc., under the editorial auspices of the Center for Research and Education in Sexuality, San Francisco State University, and the *Journal of Homosexuality*.

Nature and Causes of Homosexuality: A Philosophic and Scientific Inquiry

Compiled and Edited by Noretta Koertge, PhD

Volume 6, Number 4, Summer 1981
Journal of Homosexuality

The Haworth Press
New York

MANUSCRIPTS. Manuscripts may be submitted to John P. DeCecco, Editor, *Journal of Homosexuality,* Center for Research and Education in Sexuality, San Francisco State University, San Francisco, CA 94132. Information concerning the preparation of manuscripts may be obtained from the Editor. *Books for review purposes* should be submitted to the Editor.

The *Journal of Homosexuality* is published quarterly in Fall, Winter, Spring and Summer. Volume One was published over a two-year period: Vol. 1(1), Fall 1974; Vol. 1(2), Winter 1975-76; Vol. 1(3), Spring 1976; Vol. 1(4), Summer 1976.

BUSINESS OFFICE. All subscription and advertising inquiries should be directed to The Haworth Press, 28 East 22 Street, New York, New York 10010. Telephone (212) 228-2800.

SUBSCRIPTIONS are on an academic year, per volume basis only. Payment must be made in U.S. or Canadian funds only. $28.00 individuals, $48.00 institutions, and $65.00 libraries. Postage and handling: U.S. orders, add $1.75; Canadian orders, add $6.00 U.S. currency or $6.50 Canadian currency. Foreign orders: individuals, add $20.00; institutions, add $30.00; libraries, add $40.00 (includes postage and handling).

INDEX. An annual index to authors is included in the Summer issue of each volume of the *Journal of Homosexuality.*

CHANGE OF ADDRESS. Please notify the Subscription Department, The Haworth Press, 75 Griswold Street, Binghamton, NY 13904 of address change. Please allow six weeks for processing; *include old and new addresses,* including zip codes.

Second class postage paid at New York, New York, and at additional mailing offices.

POSTMASTER: Send address changes to The Haworth Press, 28 East 22 Street, New York, New York 10010.

Library of Congress Cataloging in Publication Data
Main entry under title:

The Nature and causes of homosexuality.

(Journal of homosexuality ; v. 6, no. 4) (Research on homosexuality ; v. 3)
Includes bibliographies and index.
1. Homosexuality—United States—Congresses. I. Koertge, Noretta. II. Series.
III. Series: Research on homosexuality ; v. 3. [DNLM: 1. Homosexuality—Congresses.
W1 J0672H v. 6 no. 4 / WM 615 N285 1979]
HQ76.3.U5N37   306.7'6   81-6960
ISBN 0-86656-148-X   AACR2

The *Journal of Homosexuality* is devoted to empirical research, and its clinical implications, on lesbianism, male homosexuality, gender identity, and alternative sexual lifestyles. It was created to serve the allied professional groups represented by psychology, sociology, anthropology, medicine, and law. Its purposes are:

 a) to bring together, within one contemporary periodical, rigorous empirical research on homosexuality and gender identity;

 b) to provide scholarly research which, although not rooted in strict experimental methodology, has heuristic value for the understanding of homosexuality and gender identity;

 c) to show the implications of these findings for helping professionals in a wide variety of disciplines and settings.

In addition, articles from the *Journal of Homosexuality* are selectively indexed or abstracted in the *ABS Guide to the Behavioral and Social Sciences, Abstracts for Social Workers, Abstracts in Anthropology, BioSciences Information Service of Biological Abstracts (BIOSIS), Le Bullétin Signaletique, Chicago Psychoanalytic Literature Index, College Student Personnel Abstracts, Criminal Justice Abstracts, Current Contents, Behavioral and Social Sciences, Excerpta Medica, Index Medicus, Index to Periodical Articles Related to Law, Pastoral Care and Counseling Abstracts, Selected List of Tables of Contents of Psychiatric Periodicals, Psychological Abstracts, Psychological Reader's Guide, Social Science Citation Index, Sociological Abstracts,* and *Women's Studies Abstracts.*

Selected articles are also cited through *CERDIC* (France), *ERIC/CAPS, International Bibliography of the Social Sciences*, and the *National Criminal Justice Reference Service (NCJRS) Index.*

Nature and Causes of Homosexuality:
A Philosophic and Scientific Inquiry

Journal of Homosexuality
Volume 6, Number 4, Summer 1981

Compiled and Edited by
Noretta Koertge, PhD

Preface   1
Noretta Koertge, PhD

Are There Gay Genes? Sociobiology and Homosexuality   5
Michael Ruse, PhD

Is Homosexuality Hormonally Determined?   35
Lynda I. A. Birke, PhD

Definition and Meaning of Sexual Orientation   51
John P. De Cecco, PhD

The Bell and Weinberg Study: Future Priorities for Research on Homosexuality   69
Frederick Suppe, PhD

Notes on the Contributors   98

INDEX TO VOLUME 6   99

Nature and Causes of Homosexuality: A Philosophic and Scientific Inquiry

PREFACE

Noretta Koertge, PhD

The theme for this special issue, *Nature and Causes of Homosexuality: A Philosophic and Scientific Inquiry,* requires some explanation. Why should philosophers of science concern themselves with research on homosexuality? And why, to put it bluntly, should sexologists be interested in what philosophers have to say? Without presuming to evaluate the success of the present interdisciplinary venture, I would like to speak about possible fruitful interactions between philosophy of science and particular scientific disciplines.

Scientists try to discover how the world works. Philosophers of science try to understand how science works. One of the aspects of science that puzzles philosophers is how a new field gets started in the first place. How do scientists decide which phenomena belong together in the same general domain? How do the theoretical concepts employed by scientists influence the way they classify data?

Such issues arise constantly in research on homosexuality. If one conceives of sex as procreation, then masturbation, homosexuality, and necrophilia all get lumped together under the heading of nonreproductive perversions, and one may seek a single explanation for all three. If one has a traditional heterosexual model for sexual activity, it is natural to look for butch/femme role-playing in homosexual relationships. If one thinks of a lesbian as someone who is "turned on" by the female body (much as are heterosexual men), it is not so farfetched to expect lesbians to adopt a male social sex role or even to have a male gender identity. However, if one conceives of a lesbian as a "woman-identified-woman," to use the modern expression, it would be implausible to expect the lesbian identity to contain extreme male elements.

Sexologists today are still groping for the most fruitful conceptualization of homosexuality (much as 18th-century chemists struggled to define acid and 19th-century biologists struggled to clarify the concept of species). It is fascinating for the philosopher who wants to understand the scientific process to follow current attempts, such as that by Shively and De Cecco, to define homosexuality.

Another vexing question for philosophers of science is the problem of ideology and metaphysics. The traditional positivistic stance would be to ban all nonempirical elements from science. Yet modern work in both the history of science and the philosophy of science seems to show that all sorts of metaphysical preconceptions, and even ideological biases, have played an important heuristic role in major scientific developments. (One recalls Copernicus' sun worship. Newton's interest in alchemy, and Einstein's determinism.)

It appears that science without metaphysics is sterile, but science dominated by untested a priori convictions becomes useless dogma. What exactly is the proper balance? Looking at actual scientific activity (and certainly research on homosexuality has had its share of problems with metaphysics and ideology) may help the philosopher arrive at a better answer.

Homosexology also raises in a particularly dramatic way methodological issues already encountered by anthropologists: To what extent can an outsider—in this case, a heterosexual man or woman—be effective in studying a different culture than her/his own? We would expect that the points of departure for heterosexual and homosexual researchers might be different, unless the homosexual researcher had totally internalized the heterosexual culture's conception of homosexuality. Certainly there is a danger of prejudice in both cases. Perhaps the scientifically preferred situation is to have a mixture of "natives" and "foreigners." If I am correct, Merton's suggestion that science is independent of "ascribed characteristics" of the researcher should be revised, but thus far, little work has been done on this metaquestion concerning the influence of backgrounds of the scientists themselves.

I have given a variety of reasons why philosophers of science should be interested in sexology, but in this issue of the *Journal*, philosophers are writing for an audience of scientists. The more relevant question is why sex researchers would be interested in essays by philosophers of science! The proof of the philosophical pudding is obviously in the reading, but perhaps it would not be too immodest to suggest some ways in which a philosopher *might* turn out to be helpful.

Philosophers are old hands at conceptual analysis. (Does *ought* imply *can*? Can reasons be causes?) Philosophers of science, working with scientists, have produced useful clarifications of the fundamental concepts and presuppositions of scientific theories. A dramatic example is the proof that the one-way velocity of light is not an empirical notion, but must be set conventionally. Philosophers of biology, on the other hand, have argued persuasively that although the evolutionary claim about survival of the fittest may appear tautological, it in fact has empirical content.

Philosophers also spend a lot of time analyzing the logical relationships among various parts of scientific systems. A classic example is Duhem's proof that Newtonian mechanics could not have been induced from Kepler's and Galileo's laws, because it is inconsistent with them. A more recent case is the demonstration that, contrary to the belief of many Darwinians, the postulation of genes for altruism is consistent with the mechanisms of natural selection.

Philosophers of science, like scientists, of course, are also extremely interested in the confirmatory and disconfirmatory relationships between hypotheses and data. However, whereas scientists often tend to make methodological criticisms of their peers privately or indirectly (e.g., "We failed to replicate Snodgrass' results"), philosophers are never happier than when trumpeting their colleagues' mistakes or omissions. (Obviously there are notable exceptions to both these generalizations.) Perhaps scientists are nicer people—more likely they think dissent is the sign of an immature science. But if Whewell was right when he said,

> The character of the true [natural] philosopher is not that he never conjectures hazardously, but that his conjectures are clearly conceived, and brought into rigid contact with facts....Truth is consistent, and can bear the tug of war: Error is incoherent, and falls to pieces in the struggle. (*Phil. of the Inductive Sciences,* 1847),

then perhaps an occasional injection of the philosopher's vitriolic candor can be salutary.

I have indicated above some ways in which philosophers of science might contribute to a scientific discipline. I certainly do not mean to suggest that philosophers have a monopoly on such activities; however, these are the sorts of things that modern philosophers of science are trained to do and enjoy doing. In the final analysis, there need be no strict division of labor between members of the two disciplines. If philosophers of science get the facts wrong about the results of scientific research, we expect to be taken sharply to task, just as scientists are expected to use valid arguments and exhibit methodological sophistication.

The articles in this special issue grew out of a symposium called *Paradigms and Prejudices in Research on Homosexuality,* which I convened at the January 1979 meeting of the American Association for the Advancement of Science in Houston. There are two exceptions. Alan Bell, who was prevented by illness from appearing at Houston, sent a reply to Suppe which was read aloud; Suppe's present paper refers to these remarks. Lynda Birke read her paper in a session on feminism and science, but it fits in perfectly with the theme of our symposium. We were amazed when officials of the AAAS informed us that never in its history had there been a session dealing with any aspect of homosexuality. Since then the situation has changed, and I am very pleased to report that at the 1980 AAAS meeting a National Organization of Lesbian and Gay Scientists was formed. (See *Science,* 1980, *209,* p. 304.)

I would like to close with an anecdote that may seem commonplace to those who spend their lives doing sex research, but which was completely novel to a philosopher of science. At our Houston symposium, after the papers and intense academic discussion were over, a little, middle-aged lady spoke to me. "My son...," she said in a deep southern accent, and for a moment I thought she might cry. Then she stood erect and spoke firmly. "I am a scientist," she said. "And today I realized that homosexuality is something which can be discussed *scientifically*. Thank you."

That, of course, is just what the *Journal of Homosexuality* is all about. Many thanks to the editors for providing us with this forum.

ARE THERE GAY GENES?
SOCIOBIOLOGY AND HOMOSEXUALITY

Michael Ruse, PhD

ABSTRACT. This paper considers recent hypotheses prepared by sociobiologists pur-
portedly giving Darwinian evolutionary explanations of human homosexuality. Four
models are considered: balanced superior heterozygote fitness, kin selection, parental
manipulation, and homosexuality as a maladaptive side effect of intensive natural selection for superior male heterosexual behavior. The evidence for the models is reviewed,
and their philosophical adequacy is considered in some depth. It is argued that although
the models pass obvious methodological hurdles and meet other criteria, as yet, the evidence for their applicability is indecisive.

Interest in human sociobiology, the study of human social behavior from
a biological viewpoint, continues at a high level. Although the controversy
and bitterness sparked by the publication of E. O. Wilson's *Sociobiology:
The New Synthesis* (1975b) seems now to be somewhat muted, the ideas and
applications of sociobiology receive increasing coverage in learned journals,
conferences, and even in the popular press. Indeed, sociobiology was
awarded that ultimate American accolade, an expository article in *Playboy*
magazine advertised as "Why Modern Science Says You Need to Cheat on
Your Wife," or some such nonsense (Morris, 1978).[1] Surely the time has
come to stop general defenses of or onslaughts on human sociobiology and
to start considering in detail specific claims made by the sociobiologists.[2] It
is at this level that the real battle must be fought if sociobiology, and particularly human sociobiology, is to prove of lasting value. Following my
own prescription, the present paper will consider sociobiologists' various
claims and suggestions about an aspect of human behavior that has
attracted quite as much interest and controversy in recent years as sociobiology itself: human homosexual inclinations and practices. An explora-
tion of sociobiologists' explanations of human homosexuality will be
followed by a critical evaluation of these ideas.

The Hypotheses

Sociobiologists do not have an "official line" on homosexuality, nor at
this stage is such a position even to be desired. Instead, the literature con-
tains a number of suggestions and hints proffered with varying degrees of

confidence and evidence. Four possible explanations of human homosexuality put forward by sociobiologists will be discussed here, although the reader is warned that at least one of these explanatory hypotheses is at this point so tentative it may be no more than half an explanation. The extent to which any or all of these explanations should be seen as excluding rival explanations is a matter to be left for later discussion.

First Hypothesis: Balanced Superior Heterozygote Fitness

The first of the sociobiological explanations sees human homosexuality as a function of balanced superior heterozygote fitness (Hutchinson, 1959). Since this explanation, like those to follow, presupposes some biological background knowledge, a sketch of such background is in order. Readers unfamiliar with biological theory might be well advised to consult Strickberger (1968). Readers are also directed toward Dobzhansky, Ayala, Stebbins, and Valentine (1977).

For evolutionary biologists, the crucial unit is the *gene*, which is carried on the chromosomes, passed on from generation to generation, and responsible in some ultimate sense for the physical characteristics of the organism. The gene's random mutation is the raw stuff of evolution.

The chromosomes of organisms, including humans, are paired. Each gene, therefore, has a corresponding gene on the other paired chromosome. Such genes are said to occupy the same *locus*; the genes that can occupy the same locus are known as *alleles*. If the alleles at some particular locus are absolutely identical, then, with respect to that locus, the organism is said to be *homozygous* (the organism is a *homozygote*). If the alleles at some particular locus are not absolutely identical, then, with respect to that locus, the organism is said to be *heterozygous* (*heterozygote*). An organism might be heterozygous with respect to one locus but homozygous with respect to another.

Organisms pass on to their offspring a copy of one, and only one, allele from each locus. The selected allele is chosen at random. In sexual organisms like humans, therefore, each parent contributes one of the alleles at any locus. This fact about transmission, known as Mendel's first law, can be generalized to groups. When applied to groups it is referred to as the Hardy-Weinberg law, after its co-discoverers. The law can be stated succinctly as follows: In the case of a large, randomly mating group of organisms, if there is no external disturbing influence, and if at some particular locus there are two alleles (A_1 and A_2) in overall proportion $p:q$, then for all succeeding generations, the proportion will remain the same. Moreover, whatever the initial distribution, over the next and all succeeding generations the alleles will be distributed in the ratio: $p^2A_1A_1 : 2pqA_1A_2 : q^2A_2A_2$ (where A_1A_1 is a homozygote for A_1, and so forth).

Now we must introduce the Darwinian element into our discussion of basic biology. Organisms have a tendency to multiply in number—think, for instance, of the millions of eggs that one female herring lays. However, this tendency is necessarily curbed; there is just not sufficient space or food for unlimited growth. The result is the struggle for existence or, more precisely, since passing on characteristics to the next generation is what counts in the evolutionary scheme of things, a struggle for reproduction. The genes must cause physical characteristics that will help their possessors in the struggle; otherwise, the genes' progress through the ages will be halted abruptly, and their organisms will be supplanted by organisms whose genes confer more helpful characteristics. Hence, we get a continual "selection" for organisms with better "adaptations" than others. Such organisms are said to be "fitter," because they are better at reproduction. In the long run, selection for reproductive fitness, when combined with mutation, is what biological evolution is all about.

Although selection normally implies change in gene ratios, with the fitter replacing the less fit, under special circumstances, selection can act to hold gene ratios constant and can even ensure that less fit organisms are maintained in a population. This is where balanced superior heterozygote fitness comes in. Consider a pair of alleles at a locus, and suppose the heterozygote is much fitter than either homozygote. Although the homozygotes might contribute little or nothing to each future generation, homozygotes will keep reappearing simply because, by the Hardy-Weinberg law, some of the offspring of heterozygotes are homozygotes. In certain circumstances, one can get a balance with the same ratios always holding.

Suppose that one has two alleles, A_1 and A_2, in equal ratio and that on the average, each of the heterozygotes produces two offspring, whereas each of the homozygotes produces none (i.e., the population number remains the same). With each generation, therefore, half the genes will be A_1 and half A_2 (because by definition heterozygotes have an equal ratio of genes and thus will contribute an equal ratio). However, by the Hardy-Weinberg law, the new distribution will be: $1/4A_1A_1 : 1/2A_1A_2 : 1/4A_2A_2$. In other words, as long as the situation continues, 25% of the new population will always be totally unfit A_1A_1s and 25% will be totally unfit A_1A_2s, a situation maintained by natural selection.

The application of this theory to the phenomenon of homosexuality is not that hard to see, but first let us note that balanced superior heterozygote fitness is not merely a theoretical possibility, it does have empirical confirmation. The best known case occurs in the human species. In certain black populations, as many as 5% die in childhood from sickle-cell anemia, a genetic disease. The apparent reason for the persistence of this disease is that heterozygotes for the sickle-cell gene have a natural immunity to malaria, also widespread in these populations. Because the heterozygotes

are fitter than either homozygote, the sickle-cell genes stay in the populations, and in each generation, a number of children die from anemia. (For
more details, see Ruse, 1973; see also Lewontin, 1974).

So, what about homosexuality? Two points must be noted. First, although I have been writing of genes causing physical characteristics, orthodox biological theory defines physical characteristics sufficiently broadly to
cover all aspects of an organism's makeup, including its behavior and inclinations.[3] Just as the structure of a worker-bee's wings is genetically caused,
so is its ability to make a perfectly hexagonal cell. Second, remember that
when a biologist talks of an organism being very unfit, this does not necessarily imply that the organism dies before reproducing, as does the child affected with sickle-cell anemia. A mule, although it might be tougher than
either parent, is regarded as unfit by an evolutionary biologist simply because it cannot reproduce. Despite the example of the mule, however,
many, if not most, of the cases of biological unfitness imply or entail unfitness at all levels.

Thus, biological principles dictate to organisms a sort of reproductive
imperative. When this is applied to the human organism, conflicts with traditional ethical systems are virtually unavoidable. Quite simply, what we
"ought" to do often runs counter to the biologically fittest course of action.
Much of our current ethical thinking stems from two major sources: Kan-
tian and utilitarian moral systems. Often, these two influences are mingled,
as in the generally accepted belief that we ought to treat human beings as
ends in their own right and not simply as means to the achievement of our
goals and that we should attempt to maximize happiness and minimize unhappiness for as many people as possible. Clearly, practical application of
such belief systems leads to the conclusion that there are times when one
ought to limit one's family size. For instance, it is immoral to have 10
children in India (or anywhere else, for that matter).

From a biological viewpoint, however, if one can successfully raise 10
children, this is a much better (i.e., fitter) thing to do than to raise a planned
two children. (The claim that society will benefit more from two than from
10 children and that two is therefore fitter than 10 is not pertinent or well-
taken; remember, biological fitness centers on the individual, not on the
group). In other words, what is moral and what is biologically fit are two
different notions; the biological unfitness of homosexual persons has no
implication for the moral desirability of a heterosexual life-style over that of
a homosexual, or vice versa. Indeed, given the present population explo-
sion, it is easy to argue for the moral acceptability of homosexuality.[4]

In light of this, one can think of a possible explanation for human homosexuality. Homosexual individuals are by definition attracted to members of
their own sex.[5] Homosexual couplings, of whatever nature, cannot lead to

offspring. Hence, someone who is exclusively homosexual cannot have offspring and is therefore effectively sterile, that is, biologically unfit. (Obviously, I exclude here the relatively rare phenomenon of a homosexual person achieving parenthood through artificial insemination.) One might be tempted to conclude that if homosexual men and women fail to reproduce (or reproduce less than their heterosexual counterparts), homosexuality could not possibly be inherited. However, as we have just seen, the mechanism of balanced heterozygote fitness provides a means whereby homosexual genes could be passed on even if homosexual individuals left no offspring at all!

Let us see how this might work. Suppose that homosexuality is a function of the genes and that possession of two "homosexual genes" makes a person homosexual. Let us also suppose, however, that heterozygotes, possessors of one "homosexual gene" and one "heterosexual gene," were fitter than homozygotes for "heterosexual genes"; in other words, that by one means or another, heterozygotes reproduce more than heterosexual-gene homozygotes. It then follows naturally that the existence and persistence of homosexuality is a function of superior heterozygote fitness. Moreover, the theory can easily accommodate the fact that sometimes homosexual persons reproduce. All that is necessary for the theory to work is that they reproduce less than heterosexual individuals. Also note that if one chooses from among the many estimates of the incidence of homosexuality a reasonable figure of about 5% of the total population, this can be accommodated by the theory, for 5% is the approximate figure suggested for sickle-cell anemia. (Needless to say, I draw this analogy not as proof, but simply to show that we are talking about a mechanism which could, in theory, handle the phenomenon of homosexuality.)

Second Hypothesis: Kin Selection

This is undoubtedly the most exciting of the new theoretical ideas of sociobiology, whether applied to animals or humans. It has been shown that, from a biological evolutionary viewpoint, reproduction is the crucial factor, but what precisely does this mean? First, while recognizing that ultimately everything comes back to the genes, it is important to ask what unit of reproduction above the level of the genes is most significant.[6] Until very recently, the majority of scientists, including most biologists, would have argued that in some important sense it is the species, the reproductively isolated interbreeding group, that is the basic unit of evolution. However, without disputing the species' very special position in the evolutionary scheme, scientists are stressing increasingly that the crucial unit of selection is the individual, that is, the reproduction of the individual organism is the cornerstone of evolutionary biology. Even if a characteristic is detrimental to the species, if it is advantageous to the individual in the short run, then selection will preserve it. (See Williams, 1966; Wilson, 1975b).

A second question now arises: Wherein lies the essence of the individual's reproduction? Obviously, it lies in the passing on of the individual's genes, the units of heredity. Note, however, that an individual is not going to pass on its own genes physically. Rather, it is going to pass on copies of its genes. The key fact behind the notion of kin selection is that it really does not matter where these copies come from. What does matter is that an organism be more efficient at perpetuating copies than its fellows.

Remember, however, that organisms are related to other organisms—brothers, sisters, cousins, and so forth—and that by Mendel's law, an organism and its relatives will have identical instances of alleles. Whenever an individual's relative reproduces, copies of the individual's own genes are being perpetuated. In theory, there is no reason why, under certain circumstances, selection should not promote characteristics that make an individual cut down or forego its own reproduction, so long as those same characteristics make the individual "altruistic" toward its relatives—in the sense that the individual increases the relatives' reproductive chances. This is kin selection. (See Barash, 1977; Dawkins, 1976; Hamilton, 1964a, 1964b; Wilson, 1975a.)

There is actually a little more to the story. With the exception of identical twins, a person is more closely related to her/himself than to anyone else. One has 100% of one's own genes; one's parents, siblings, and offspring have 50% of one's genes; grandchildren 25%, first cousins 12.5%; and so forth. Hence, under normal circumstances one will prefer the reproduction of oneself even over close relatives.[7] Simple arithmetic shows, for instance, that if by foregoing one's own reproduction one thereby increases a sibling's reproduction by over 100%, then it is in one's own reproductive interest to do so, for more copies of one's own genes are thereby transmitted. More generally, if k is the ratio of gain to loss in fitness and if r is the coefficient of relationship of benefiting relatives ($0 < r < 1$), then for kin selection to work, $k > 1/r$ (i.e., if C is cost and B benefit, $C < rB$).

Kin selection is not only exciting theoretically. Its application to the social insects, although still controversial in some respects, is one of the triumphs of sociobiology. The Hymenoptera (wasps, bees, ants) show a distinctive, tight social structure, with hordes of sterile females altruistically raising their mother's (i.e., the queen's) offspring, the males, incidentally, doing no work at all. It is now believed that this is a function of kin selection. (See Oster & Wilson, 1978).

It is easy to see how an analysis like this would tempt sociobiologists faced with the phenomenon of human homosexuality (Weinrich, 1976; Wilson, 1975b). Assuming that homosexual individuals have fewer offspring than heterosexual individuals, their apparent loss of reproductive fitness could be "exonerated" in terms of the increased fitness of close relatives. All one needs to do is to postulate that homosexual men and women take altruistic or high-prestige jobs such as the priesthood, act as unpaid nannies to the children of siblings, etc. Thus, the siblings (or other relatives) gain in reproductive power and so, indirectly, do the homosexual individuals. If this explanation were true, homosexual humans would be analogous to sterile worker-bees in that they reproduce through relatives rather than directly.

Simple and obvious though this explanatory hypothesis may be, it raises even more simple and obvious queries, not the least being those concerning the imputed altruistic motives and actions.

Third Hypothesis: Parental Manipulation

The key to kin selection is that it does not really matter how one's genes get passed on; what is evolutionarily important is that one increase or at least maintain one's genetic representation in future generations. Parental manipulation presupposes a similar attitude to the workings of natural selection and, likewise, serves to explain human homosexuality in terms of genetically caused altruism. The difference, however, is that whereas the kin-selection explanation regards homosexuality as a form of altruism ultimately of benefit to the nonreproducing homosexual individual, parental manipulation sees homosexuality as a form of altruism which ultimately benefits others, namely, the homosexual individual's parents (Trivers, 1974). Alexander (1971, 1974, 1975) has most strongly endorsed the general mechanism of parental manipulation, but, as will be shown, he seems to prefer a different primary mechanism for (male) human homosexuality.

Speaking generally and as yet unconcerned with homosexuality specifically, let us first examine the essentials of the supposed mechanism of parental manipulation. Consider an organism with a number of offspring. Clearly, it is in the organism's reproductive self-interest to have its offspring reproduce as efficiently as possible. Although the organism's reproductive interests depend on its offspring as a whole, it is not necessarily true that these interests are identical with any one of the offspring taken individually. Indeed, if an organism has more than one offspring, then the parent's interest will not be the same as any individual offspring, for remember that even a parent and its child have only 50% of their genes in common.[8] Consequently, considering a parent organism with a number of offspring, there may be occasions when it is in the parent's reproductive interest to sacrifice one or more of its offspring for the benefits that would accrue to the other offspring. Suppose, for example, that if all the offspring were to pursue their own interests, then only one would survive and in turn reproduce. Suppose also, however, that if one of the offspring were no longer to compete for itself, then as a result, two of its siblings would survive to reproduce. Clearly, this latter situation is not in the interests of the noncompetitive offspring, which is substituting a zero chance of reproductive success for what had been at least a minimally positive chance. (The qualification "under normal circumstances" is required because obviously kin selection might also come into play.)

It would seem, therefore, that if the genes could give rise to behavior in one or both parents that would in some way and under special circumstances cause one offspring to become a nonreproducer, and this were in the parent's reproductive interests, such genes would be preserved and even multiplied by selection. Obviously, the circumstances would have to be rather special. Normally, if a parent would be better off with fewer potentially reproductive children, its best reproductive strategy would be not to have surplus offspring in the first place. However, another way to bring about the same situation would be for the parent's genetically caused behavior to force one offspring not merely not to compete with its siblings, but to aid the siblings in their reproductive quest. If the behavior could induce such altruism, it might well pay a parent to have an extra offspring, even though the offspring would never itself reproduce. This, then, is the essence of parental manipulation, although it must be pointed out that, despite the language, sociobiologists do not mean to imply conscious manipulative intent on the part of the parent. Indeed, the mechanism might well be more effective if both parent and child were unaware of what was going on.

The mechanism of parental manipulation has not met with unqualified enthusiasm, even from otherwise committed sociobiologists (see Dawkins, 1976). Nevertheless, there seem to be at least some cases in the animal world where parental manipulation actually occurs. The phenomenon of so-called trophic eggs, where, at times of drought or famine, some offspring are fed to others, would seem to qualify as an example.

At this point, and without concerning ourselves too greatly with the question of evidence, let us turn to the more specific question of how parental manipulation might be proposed as a mechanism for human homosexuality. One has merely to suppose that in some way, when it is in a parent's reproductive interests, this parent's behavior could cause a child to switch from developing into an exclusively heterosexual adult to developing into a person with at least some homosexual inclinations and practices. In our era, soaked as we are in Freudian and neo-Freudian speculations, to suppose that a parent can "make a child homosexual" does not require much of a leap of the imagination; to many, it is almost common sense. One must of course assume, as in the case of kin selection, that the homosexual individual is indeed aiding its siblings or close relatives.

According to this view, therefore, homosexual men and women are not born, they are made—by the parents. There are, of course, genetic requirements, too: The parent must have genes that cause homosexuality-producing behavior; the offspring must have genes that permit it to be diverted into a homosexual role.

Fourth Hypothesis: Homosexuality as a By-Product

The fourth and final hypothesis hardly merits the title "explanation"; it is simply an unpublished speculation by one of the leading sociobiologists. However, given the fact that one philosopher of science has responded warmly to the idea and given that it does rather complete a list of the obvious possible ways in which homosexuality could be explained biologically, it seems worthwhile and legitimate briefly to consider the idea. It must be remembered that here we really are in the realm of speculation.[9]

Basically this explanation, credited to Richard Alexander, understands homosexuality (or more particularly, male homosexuality) as a by-product of, or as an incidental to, normal heterosexual development. Alexander writes: "It seems to me that an inadequately explored angle, in terms of immediate causes, is the idea that something which selected powerfully for heterosexual success (i.e., reproduction) incidentally renders us all capable of homosexual preference, given particular circumstances especially during development." He goes on to suggest that males compete very intensely for females (more so than females for males) and that just as one of the effects of this competition is that males have higher mortality than females and are more prone to disease and aging—"maladaptive, inevitable concomitants of the higher-stakes, higher-risk male strategy"—so too, "novel or extreme circumstances might be more likely to yield behavior (like homosexuality) that actually prevents (reproductive) success."

Rather than postulating genes directly linked with homosexuality, as was the case in each of the first three hypotheses discussed, Alexander suggests that some feature which ordinarily would enhance an individual's ability to compete in the struggle to reproduce could, in special circumstances, also divert that individual into homosexuality.

Now what could such a feature be? What sort of attribute might usually lead to reproductive success but occasionally sidetrack one into homosexuality? Alexander's candidate is the propensity to masturbate! (Many 19th-century sexologists must be happily nodding approval in their graves.) Alexander points out that for most people, and particularly for boys, initial sexual experiences are autosexual: That is to say, boys masturbate a lot. The point here is that, absolutely, boys masturbate a fair amount and, relatively, masturbate more than do girls. Masturbation in adolescence seems normally to be of adaptive significance: One is learning about sex. For boys, however, there lurks the possibility of being switched towards homosexuality. After all, the masturbator is playing with organs of his own sex, and the visual stimuli are much more obvious for males than females. An erect penis, even if it is one's own, catches the eye far more than an erect clitoris, especially if it is one's own. Thus the male, as part of normal heterosexual development, treads a fine line between heterosexuality and homosexuality.

> We know that males masturbate more than females (both very likely are concomitants of more intense sexual competition). Moreover, male masturbation provides visual as well as tactual stimuli that are very similar to those involved in some homosexual activities. If one is stimulated sexually a great deal by seeing his own erect penis, then to be sexually stimulated by seeing someone else's is not such a great leap. Even if tactual and other stimuli are not greatly different between the sexes (and they may actually be), this great difference in visual feedback seems to be potentially quite significant.

Does our society have any idiosyncracies that push males towards homosexuality? Indeed it does, namely, the fact that because so many males must wait so long before they can have heterosexual experiences, their only sexual relief is masturbation. By the time full heterosexual possibilities are available, it may be too late: The masturbating males prefer penises to vaginas. Thus, as a result of changes in society unrelated to sexuality, males are pushed towards homosexuality.

Alexander writes:

> Now, given the above sexual differences, and the likelihood (again, *somewhat* speculative) of enormous importance of *initial sexual experience*, what's going to happen if society creates a situation in which practically all boys masturbate for years before they have a real heterosexual experience? It seems to me that, for *incidental* reasons, many of them will become predominantly or solely homosexuals, and another large complement may continue to rely on masturbation as a sexual outlet, and may actually teeter on the edge of homosexuality as well. Females would not be so greatly affected.

Concluding this discussion, Alexander suggests that women have more trouble grasping the possible connection between masturbation and homosexuality, presumably because no such connection obtains in women's sexual development.

The Evidence

It is now time to ask: Are any of these four possible sociobiological accounts of homosexuality true? How much evidence is there for or against each of them at present? What new data should be collected in order to test them?

Because the sociobiology of homosexuality is so new, many of the pertinent studies remain undone. Empirical science is not a question of simply gathering information, but rather of gathering information in the light of some hypothesis. Until recently, we did not have the sociobiological hypotheses. Now that we do, we can begin empirical studies in earnest, although for the time being we may have to make theoretical bricks with very little empirical straw.

Balanced Superior Heterozygote Fitness

This is still very much a hypothesis and appears to have been proposed for no better reason than because it describes one way to generate less than biologically fit humans. As yet, no study has shown that over a number of generations the ratios and distributions of homosexual to heterosexual offspring match those to be expected were a balanced superior heterozygote fitness mechanism at work. Indeed, it is questionable just how biologically unfit homosexuality actually is. It may be logical to suggest that a man who is attracted to other men will have fewer children than one who is exclusively heterosexual, but many homosexual men have fathered children. How reproductively unfit are homosexual men in our society? How unfit are they in preliterate societies?

Another problem is raised by the existence and nature of women. Fairly central to sociobiological theorizing is the claim that females (excluding fish but including humans) have little command over whether or not they will reproduce (Trivers & Willard, 1973). Males must compete for females, and hence, many males do not reproduce. Females, however, although they can use certain strategies to get a good mate, tend to be fertilized come what may. Does this imply, as there is empirical evidence to suggest, that lesbians are biologically as fit as their heterosexual sisters? This would not mean that, overall, homosexuality could not be biologically deleterious; the situation would approximate that of a sex-associated characteristic like hemophilia, which appears almost invariably in the male. It would mean, however, that theoretical ratios would change, and one would expect to find empirical evidence thereof.

In short, the balance hypothesis for homosexuality seems little more than a hypothesis, but before abandoning it altogether, one other area of possible evidence should be examined—evidence that may provide some necessary, albeit insufficient, conditions for the truth of the balance hypothesis. I refer to evidence that might be expected to show whether or not homosexuality is a genetic trait (Hull, 1978).

It is commonly thought (i.e., by nonbiologists) that there is a fairly rigid dichotomy between genetically caused traits or characteristics and environmentally caused traits. Much of the controversy over the causes of intelligence has resulted from the belief that IQ is either a matter of *nature*, something one inherits, or a matter of *nurture*, something one is educated to or otherwise environmentally forced into. As biologists now realize, however, this sharply conceived dichotomy is misleading. All characteristics are in some sense a function of the genes in interaction with the environment. There is virtually nothing that could not be changed by a change in the genes; similarly, there is virtually nothing that could not be changed by a change in the environment. Why am I taller than my father? Partially because my mother's family members are taller than my father's. Partially because (English) children were better fed during the Second World War than they were during the First.

Nevertheless, some characteristics, such as human eye color, are controlled more by the genes in the sense that these characteristics develop on certain pathways, regardless of the normal environmental fluctuations. Conversely, some characteristics, such as speaking English rather than French, are more under the control of the environment in that they are very sensitive to variations in the normal environment, especially during development. If genetic and environmental traits are understood in these qualified senses, it would seem that a presupposition of the balance hypothesis for human homosexuality is that homosexuality falls fairly close to the genetic end of the spectrum. The hypothesis supposes that almost inevitably a homozygote for the homosexual gene will be homosexual and not otherwise.[10]

The question to be asked, therefore, is whether homosexuality is genetic in this sense. Note that a positive finding only provides a necessary condition for the truth of the hypothesis. A characteristic can be essentially genetically controlled in many ways other than through homozygosity for a recessive gene. One could have straightforward dominance of a homosexual gene. Even if it were established that the pertinent causative gene is recessive, this does not prove, as the balance hypothesis claims, that the heterozygote is superior in fitness to all of the homozygotes.

To discover if homosexuality is genetic, one needs to observe situations where one might hope to distinguish genetic from environmental conditions. An experimental situation of growing popularity, particularly with those concerned with the genetics of IQ, is provided by adoption.[11] If one can trace adopted children and their biological and adoptive parents, then one can observe if the children are more like their biological parents, in which case the genes seem to be playing the crucial role, or more like their adoptive parents, in which case the environment seems to be reigning. Unfortunately, in the case of homosexuality, it is not that easy to know to what extent studies of adoption would be applicable. Certainly many homosexual men and women have reproduced; but, as explained earlier, by the very nature of the case the data will be limited because homosexual individuals will tend to be less than fully reproductive. Also, I would imagine that gathering the required information would not be easy. A woman giving up a child for adoption might be prepared to answer questions about the education and jobs of herself and her lover. She might be far less willing to tell all about their sexual inclinations and practices. (Would a pregnant teenager know or admit that her boyfriend was homosexual? Even if she or her boyfriend had had homosexual encounters, how reliable a guide would that be to their adult sexual orientation?)

Much more promising are twin tests. There are two kinds of sets of twins: monozygotic twins, who share the same genotype, and dizygotic twins, who do not and are therefore no more closely related than normal siblings (i.e., 50%). If one finds a significant divergence between the differences between monozygotic twins and the differences between dizygotic twins, then, since generally both twins experience the same environment, a reasonable inference is that genetic factors are involved. There is one major study of this kind, and the results, taken on their own, are astoundingly impressive (Kallmann, 1952; Heston & Shields, 1968). In a study by Kallmann of 85 sets of twins where at least one twin showed homosexual behavior, in all 50 monozygotic cases, both twins were homosexual and, moreover, homosexual to much the same intensity. In the dizygotic cases, on the other hand, most of the twins of homosexual individuals showed little or no homosexual inclination or behavior. One could not ask for stronger evidence of a genetic component to human homosexuality. Indeed, the evidence is so strong one is reminded of Mendel's too perfect figures confirming his pea plant experiments.

Against Kallmann's study it must be noted that since then, cases of monozygotic twins with different sexual orientations have been discovered (e.g., Rainer, Mesnikoff, Kolb, & Carr, 1960). It certainly does seem that homosexuality has some genetic basis, that it is not exclusively a function of environmental factors. Apart from anything else, it is almost inconceivable that the basic human sex drive, whatever its orientation, would have no genetic causal component. Humans would very soon die out if none of us cared a fig for sex or if we were attracted to cabbages rather than fellow humans. So at a maximum it would seem that, given our genetic sexuality, the environment could establish our preference for members of the same sex or the opposite sex, although no doubt the environment might increase or decrease the strength of our sexuality.

The counterfindings suggest two, not necessarily incompatible, possibilities. The first is that there are multiple causes of homosexuality. Perhaps some forms of homosexuality are essentially a function of the genes, whereas other forms or manifestations require a significant environmental input. Genetically speaking, this is quite plausible. Suppose homosexuality were a function of the number of genes, i.e., if one had more than a certain number, then homosexuality would inevitably appear, but if one had less than that number, then a specific environmental input would be required to cause homosexuality. A person with none of the genes would not be homosexual whatever the input. This is a well-known phenomenon.[12] The second possibility is that at least one form of homosexuality has a genetic base but still requires some kind of special environmental input. Without it, one is heterosexual. (Alternatively, some form or manifestation of heterosexuality might require some kind of special environmental input; without it, one is homosexual.)

It should be added that some of the reported counterexamples to Kallmann's study (i.e., monozygotic twins with different sexual orientations) lend plausibility to one or the other of the above possibilities, both of which require some specific environmental input to produce homosexuality. In the reported cases, there is evidence that within each pair, the twins were treated differently, with the later-to-be-homosexual twin generally getting more mothering, being treated more like a girl (nearly all the cases are of males), and so forth (Rainer et al., 1960).

In short, the evidence from twin tests provides fairly strong support for the belief that the genes play some role in homosexuality, although there is also evidence that the environment plays an important role. This brings us full circle back to Freud, for this was precisely his belief (Freud, 1905)! As pointed out, however, this conclusion does not support the balanced superior heterozygote fitness hypothesis as such, although the evidence is certainly compatible with other genetic mechanisms. Moreover, there are findings of another sort which cast doubt on the balance hypothesis. These are statistical findings about birth orders and parental ages at birth of child. In particular, there are significant correlations between male homosexuality and birth order (younger sons have a greater tendency to be homosexual) and between male homosexuality and age of parent at birth (older parents have more homosexual sons). At one point it was thought that the main correlation was between older mothers and homosexual sons, but now it seems that the age of the mother is a function of the age of the father, although indeed mothers are older.[13]

Now, if homosexuality were a simple case of balanced superior heterozygote fitness, these findings should not obtain. There is nothing in normal

Mendelian theory, on which the balance hypothesis rests, to account for them. Indeed, an older child would be just as likely to be a homosexual homozygote as would older parents. At the very least, the findings suggest either that there are causes of homosexuality other than a balance mechanism or that the balance mechanism is complicated by other factors, genetic or environmental. At this point, given the lack of positive evidence for the balance mechanism and given the existence of other hypotheses, judicious use of Occam's razor is in order.

One might think that these findings about parental age and so forth would be fatal to any genetic hypothesis about the etiology of homosexuality, but this is not necessarily so. First, as has been noted, there might be multiple causes of homosexuality. Some homosexuality could be fairly directly controlled by the genes, and some not so. Although the above correlations point to significant connections between homosexuality, low birth order, and high parental age, they certainly do not deny that some homosexual men and women are first-born or that some have young parents. Second, it is well established that some genetic phenomena are a function of parental age (which is possibly not entirely unconnected with birth order, although not directly causally connected). In particular, the ova and sperm of older people are much more likely than those of younger people to have mutated in certain ways. For instance, older mothers are much more prone to having children afflicted with Down's syndrome (mongolism), caused by an extra chromosome, and older fathers are more prone to children with hemophilia (Hilton, Callahan, Harris, Condliffe, & Berkley, 1973). There is, however, no cytological evidence for this hypothesis as it might apply in the case of homosexuality (see Marmor, 1965).

Third, and perhaps most likely, the correlations are compatible with a genetic hypothesis if the environment also plays a significant causal role. The correlations suggest a more protective attitude of the parents (particularly the mother) than is usual and also a child who feels cowed and dominated (and perhaps protected) by older siblings. Furthermore, an older father may play a less active role than usual. It is easy to see how environmental input of this kind could trigger a homosexual orientation in a child who already has the requisite genes. This would also explain why not all younger children or children of older parents are homosexual—most are not! For that matter, we would then have an explanation for why all children of dominant mothers (or whatever the environmental input may be) are not homosexual; they, too, lack the required genes.

I suggest, therefore, that our discussion so far has shown that at least some homosexuality could have a genetic component in the sense explicated above, that it is highly improbable that the environment does not play an important role, that the environmental input might be connected to familial factors such as parental age and birth order, and that while the balance hypothesis has not been proven false, it is unlikely to be the exclusive source of human homosexuality—indeed, its only recommendation is that it is one way to get reduced fertility (which, it is assumed, homosexual individuals have).

Kin Selection

The key equation for the operation of kin selection, it will be remembered, is $C < rB$, where C is the reproductive *cost*, or loss of one's own personal reproductive success; r is one's degree of *relatedness* to the person who benefits; and B is the reproductive *benefit* conferred on the recipient of altruism. Thus, for instance, one's full siblings ($r = 1/2$) must benefit more than twice as much as one loses. There are a number of ways in which this inequality might obtain or be made more likely: if one's personal chances of reproduction are low, if the relationship to the recipient is high, and if the benefits obtained are high.

When applying this theory to homosexuality, it is assumed that homosexual individuals reduce their own reproductive fitness in order to boost the fitness of close relatives, especially siblings. There need not be anything intentional about this, but the effect is that in being homosexual, offspring become altruistic towards close relatives in order thereby to increase their own overall "inclusive fitness." This explanation is genetic in that the homosexual potential exists, but environmental in that the potential requires some reason to be triggered. (Since we are not Hymenoptera, there is no a priori advantage to being homosexual.) In verifying this hypothesis, one would look for some environmental reason suggesting, not necessarily consciously, that heterosexuality would be a bad reproductive strategy. In this, the kin selection hypothesis differs from the balance hypothesis. It differs also in expecting the homosexual individual to be altruistic: Family members must breed better because of a relative's homosexual life-style.

A number of sociobiologists have suggested that a major key to the causes of human homosexuality may lie in this theory of kin selection, and recent James Weinrich has argued the thesis at some length, basing his study on a far more detailed and extensive search of the empirical literature than had ever been undertaken before (Weinrich, 1976; see also Wilson, 1978). In line with another position taken by many sociobiologists and described above, Weinrich believes that the most unbiased sources of evidence for possible genetic foundations of human homosexuality lie in "primitive" or preliterate societies, for these most closely approximate early societies when natural selection was having its fullest effects on humans. With respect to homosexuality, Weinrich believes some suggestive extrapolations between preliterate societies and our own are possible.

Now, there are many reports in the anthropological literature of homosexuality of various forms in preliterate societies. One reads of various kinds of cross-dressing involving homosexual intercourse and even, in some societies, of certain forms of homosexual marriage. Unfortunately, because many of the reports concern adulthood almost exclusively, there is little information on whether something had occurred during the childhood of the homosexual adult which would make adult homosexuality an attractive reproductive strategy.

What information there is, however, suggests that adopting a homosexual life-style frequently follows or is accompanied by phenomena that would indeed lower the reproductive cost. For instance, at one time among the Araucans of South America, all ritualized homosexual males "were men who had taken up the role of women, who took 'the passive role' in homosexual relations, and who were chosen for the role in childhood, due to their feminine mannerisms or certain physical deformities" (Weinrich, 1976, p. 170). Among the Nuer, a "woman who marries another woman is usually barren" (p. 171). Among the Toradjas, the male homosexual life-style and women's work occurred "primarily because of cowardice or some harrowing experience" (p. 171). Generally, ritualized homosexual roles seem "to be attractive to individuals who have undergone some trauma, regardless of whether this involves a change of sex" (p. 173), although there certainly are exceptions. From a biological point of view, if such individuals have a low expectation of having offspring anyway, they have little to lose by becoming homosexual. In fact, if their siblings have more children as a result, they have much to gain.

Our own society provides some evidence to back up low C (reproductive cost) or low probability of C for homosexual individuals. "In accounts of modern male-to-female transsexuals, it is very common to read of some sort of childhood trauma immediately preceding the appearance of femininity" (Weinrich, 1976, p. 173). A study of a group of effeminate boys (who apparently have a much higher probability of turning out homosexual than do average boys) "showed an above-average incidence of certain physical defects" (p. 173). Two other pieces of information may be pertinent, although Weinrich does not argue from them directly. First, a careful study implied that there are fairly significant physical differences between adult homosexual and adult heterosexual males. On the average (i.e., there are definite exceptions), heterosexual males are heavier, although not taller, by 6.25 kilos and are stronger. As a statistical ensemble, homosexual males "had less subcutaneous fat and smaller muscle/bone development and were longer in proportion to bulk. Their shoulders were narrower in relation to pelvic width, and their muscle strength was less" (Weinrich, 1976, p. 129). Given the fairly strong links between child development and the adult state, one might suppose that as a group, future homosexual males comprise the slighter, weaker children who face the possibility of reduced C, making a homosexual strategy more attractive from a biological viewpoint. (This would be especially true in preliterate societies.) Incidentally, lesbians tend to be taller than heterosexual females; would it make sense to suggest that this reduces their C also? Second, it should be remembered that homosexual children tend to be lower down in birth order. A lower birth order might not be so significant in our own society, but elsewhere this could be a reproductive handicap. By the time the youngest child comes along, most of the family resources, e.g., a family farm, may already have been appropriated, significantly lowering the child's potential reproductive cost. Simply out of reproductive self-interest, it would pay the youngest child not to enter into heterosexual competition. All in all, therefore, it would seem that there is some evidence of lowered C or potential C for homosexual individuals.

At this point, there must be grumblings (or shrieks) of discontent from some readers. "Homosexuals are being presented as sickly, reedy little runts, unable to measure up to their heterosexual siblings! If this is not stereotypic thinking, nothing is." In reply to this objection, two points can be made. First, thanks to modern medicine, in our society, someone who has had a childhood disease can be as perfectly physically fit as an adult. Second, there is nothing vilifying of homosexual men and women in the facts just related. If heterosexual men are indeed heavier and stronger than homosexual men, that is simply a fact. (Before accepting it as a universal truth, however, I would need the evidence of many more empirical studies.) Moreover, if sociobiologists want to seize upon such a fact and use it to explain human sexual orientation, that is their right. After all, homosexuality must have *some* cause, and in terms of logic, having smaller body weight seems on a par with having a dominant mother, to cite a cause favored by many analysts. Certainly, smaller body weight is just the sort of thing that would attract evolutionists, which is what sociobiologists are, after all. If evolutionists found two races of the same species of animal with significant body-weight differences, they would feel an explanation was in order and would search for other differences and consequences.[14]

So far we have considered only one side of the equation. The crucial inequality for kin selection is $C < rB$. Although this can be achieved by lowering C, raising B also helps. (I assume we are dealing with a fairly high r.) If a kin selection hypothesis for human homosexuality is to have any plausibility, then we might very reasonably expect to find that B, the amount one can help one's relatives, will be higher than normal. If one persists in linking facts to values, the values here would seem to elevate the status of homosexual men and women.

Again, consulting the example of preliterate societies, Weinrich argues that in such societies, homosexual persons tend to have high status which presumably would redound to the credit of close relatives. Weinrich documents the fact that in society after society, certain individuals adopt the dress and roles of members of the opposite sex, perform tasks appropriate to that sex, and engage in relations with members of their own sex. Moreover, with very few exceptions, homosexual persons have high status within their societies and, because they are considered to have certain special magical or religious powers, they often act as priests or "shamans." Weinrich (1976, pp. 203-205) catalogues their dignity thus: among the W. Inoits, "advice always followed"; the Araucans, "advice required for every important decision"; the Cheyenne, "goes to war; matchmaker; supervises scalps and scalp ceremonies"; the Illinois, "required for all important decisions"; the Navaho, "wealthy; leaders, mediators; matchmakers; unusual opportunity for material advancement"; the Sioux, "extraordinary privileges"; the Sea Dyaks, "rich; persons of great consequence; often chief." In short, being homosexual and taking on a homosexual role in such societies often led to very high status and consequent opportunity to advance the cause and comforts of close relatives; that is, homosexual offspring were specially suited to raising the reproductive chances of those who shared their genes, for they could confer a high B on their relatives, which is something else required for the efficient operation of kin selection.

Of course, in our own society it is hardly true to say that homosexual men or women have an elevated status. Indeed, they tend to be despised and persecuted.[15] There does seem to be some evidence, however, that they have special abilities that would fit well in the roles which they would have been expected to play in preliterate societies where, according to sociobiologists, natural selection would have been having its crucial influence. Indeed, the abilities might even be such as to raise the B of homosexual persons in our own society, despite their apparent low status.

For one thing, there is evidence that they tend to have greater acting ability than heterosexual people (Weinrich, 1976, p. 175). Of course, it is notorious in our society that the stage (as do the arts generally) has a far higher proportion of homosexual participants than, say, the teaching profession. It could be that they are attracted to the stage precisely because this is one area where they will be accepted as normal. (Indeed, there are cases of heterosexuals who behave homosexually for the sake of professional advancement within the theater.) There is evidence that homosexuality has an even more complex causal relationship with the dramatic flair. For instance, effeminate boys, a group with proportionately more future homosexual adults than average, "are unusually adept at stage-acting and role-taking—at an age long before they could know that the acting profession has an unusually high incidence of homosexuality" (Weinrich, 1976, p. 175). In other words, there is at least the possibility of a genetic link between homosexuality and acting ability, that is, between some homosexuality and some acting ability.

It is obvious that the ability to act would be of value to a priest or shaman, given that so much of their work centers on magic, mysteries, and ceremonies.

The other pertinent piece of information is that homosexual individuals tend to have a higher IQ than their heterosexual peers. Several studies support this claim (Weinrich, 1976, p. 176). Of course, the whole question of intelligence and IQ tests gets one into some very murky areas, and some of the more grandiose and pernicious claims have been very properly criticized. Nevertheless, three pertinent points can be made. First, increasingly there is evidence that intelligence of some form exists and that this shares some kind of causal link with the genes—not, I rush to say, independent of the environment; indeed, this kin selection argument rather invokes the environment.[16] Second, the justifiable criticisms of IQ studies, on the grounds that many are sexually or racially biased, are irrelevant to homosexual studies for which the comparison groups were drawn from similar social, sexual, and racial groups.

Third, and most importantly, the fear that IQ does not really represent some absolute quality of "brightness," but more an ability to get on in society (and to do well on things that teachers value, like IQ tests!) supports the kin selection hypothesis rather than detracts from it. Apparently, almost anyone can raise children, although some do it better than others. What homosexual persons must do, given the kin selection hypothesis, is raise themselves in society to such an extent that they win benefits for their kin, e.g., through influence, find good jobs for nephews and nieces. In other words, homosexual men and women need to possess just those abilities and attitudes that critics fear are reflected on IQ tests. If society demands conformity rather than ingenuity, if the tests measure the former rather than the latter, if homosexual individuals shine on the tests, so much the better for the kin selection hypothesis.

Weinrich suggests that the increased abilities of homosexual people may be the effects of modifier genes. Perhaps a child has a physical injury. This affects its potential C. The child's genes then switch the child towards a homosexual orientation, and modifier genes come into play to increase the child's potential B. It would seem, however, that things could also work the other way, that children with certain superior abilities would be switched towards homosexuality in order that their inclusive fitness might be increased. It is important to emphasize that genes are pretty "ruthless." The case of the Hymenoptera clearly illustrates that there is nothing biologically sacred about parenthood. If it is in the reproductive interests of an organism to breed vicariously, then so be it. It is biologically possible that in humans, with their newly evolved factor of high intelligence, such reproduction by proxy could be a very attractive option.

How convincing is the evidence for the kin selection hypothesis for human homosexuality? Although most nonbiologists, and for that matter a good many biologists, find it difficult to take seriously any kind of kin selection hypothesis, I think that our experience with the Hymenoptera shows kin selection to be sensible and a crucial tool in causal understanding of animal sociality. Furthermore, since humans are animals, we ought at least to consider kin selection as working, or as having worked, on the human genotype. I suggest, therefore, that a case has been made for taking seriously the hypothesis that at least some human homosexuality may be a causal function of the operation of kin selection, if not in our own society, then in the societies of our ancestors.

On the other hand, no definitive case has been made for the hypothesis as yet. For instance, no proof has yet been offered showing that homosexual offspring really do increase the fitness of their relatives and thus, indirectly, increase their own inclusive fitness. Is it indeed the case that siblings of homosexual individuals successfully rear more offspring than they would have otherwise? It would be interesting to know, even in our own society, what attitudes homosexual men and women have towards their siblings and their nephews and nieces. Is there evidence, e.g., in the form of money left in wills, that they help their relatives to reproduce? Similarly, much more work needs to be done on the nature of homosexual people themselves. Do we systematically find that their C or potential C is reduced or had been reduced in childhood? In short, the case seems "not proven." Conversely, it ought to be taken seriously by anyone interested in the etiology of human homosexuality.

Parental Manipulation

In certain respects, this hypothesis overlaps the kin selection hypothesis, and much of the evidence garnered for one applies equally to the other. For instance, if a child has reduced C or potential C, it might be in the interest of the parents, and the child, to direct the child towards homosexuality. Similarly, if the homosexual offspring can and do benefit their relatives, this will help the parents as well as the children. Weinrich's evidence about the causes of shamanism and the status of shamans applies to this hypothesis as well as to the kin selection hypothesis.

The two hypotheses, however, are not identical and can lead to different predictions. What is in the reproductive interests of the parents might not be in the reproductive interests of the child. If a parent has three children and each child raises two children, there will be six grandchildren. Suppose, however, that one child were a nonreproductive altruist, then the others could raise three more children between them. Such altruism would benefit the parent, who would then have seven grandchildren instead of six, but would not benefit the altruist, who would exchange two children for three nephews or nieces, i.e., $2 \times 50\%$ of its own genes for $3 \times 25\%$ of its own genes. More generally, conflict arises between parent and child over help to siblings, at a C to the child, whenever $C < B < 2C$. Therefore, by identifying cost/benefit ratios, one ought to be able to distinguish between the operation of kin selection and parental manipulation or to recognize the presence of both.

Unfortunately, because we as yet have no quantified statistics on the benefits of having a homosexual sibling, there is presently no direct way to distinguish between kin selection and parental manipulation. What we can do, however, is to ask if there is evidence that parents actively mold or influence their children, consciously or unconsciously, into homosexual lifestyles. This must occur if the hypothesis of parental manipulation is to have any truth at all.

In fact, the anthropological evidence is very strong that parents do play such a positive role. In case after case of homosexuality in preliterate societies, as listed by Weinrich (1976), the parents play a part in encouraging or permitting the child to move towards the status of a member of the opposite sex. For instance, among the Sea Dyaks, in order to take on the cross-gender role of a *manang bali,* "one's father must pay a series of increasing fees to initiate the grown son into the role, and all three investigators (of the phenomenon) agree that the *manang bali* are invariably rich (often chiefs) as a result of their fees for shamanizing" (p. 169). Similarly, in societies where a high bride price is demanded, parents will sometimes shift sons toward a female role, thereby changing an economic liability into an asset.

One might protest that the very opposite is the case in our own society. Most parents recoil from the thought of having a homosexual child. However, apart from the fact that our society may be atypical and inconsequential to long-range evolutionary considerations, it must be remembered that conscious manipulation is not demanded by sociobiology; indeed, control may be more effective if it occurs unrecognized. It is certainly tempting to speculate that when faced with a child who suffers some illness, parents become extraordinarily protective, thus triggering or aiding a switch in future sexual orientation. Again, if there is indeed anything to this whole question of birth order and the age of parents, it is not difficult to see how this might support parental manipulation. As the family gets larger and larger and, coincidentally, as the parents grow older; it becomes more in the parents' interest to raise a child to be altruistic towards the other children, rather than as yet another competitor. So, unwittingly, the mother smothers her youngest with affection, thus turning the child to homosexuality. Conversely, the father may start to lose interest, with the same effect occurring. This, of course, is all very speculative, intended merely to suggest that the parental manipulation hypothesis, like the kin selection hypothesis, deserves further study.

By-Product of Intense Male Heterosexual Competition

This is but a speculative and hitherto unpublished idea, and, as might be expected, it is not yet supported by much hard evidence. How could one test Alexander's suggestion that male homosexuality is a function of intense selection for heterosexual ability gone haywire? Certainly one could test the initial, crucial premise that competition among males is more intense than among females. Moreover, if the premise were true, then by implication there would be significant measurable differences between female homosexuality and male homosexuality—differences that transcend fairly obvious physiological differences, e.g., because males do not have vaginas but do have penises, almost necessarily homosexual males are going to be more anally oriented than lesbians.[17] One could also test whether homosexual males are in some ways more aggressive, perhaps more promiscuous, than homosexual females. Of course, Alexander's suggestion does not tackle female homosexuality. One must first invoke some other explanation for lesbianism and then see what the various implications for the possible differences between the female and male homosexualities would be.

The other significant way in which Alexander's suggestion seems to open itself to test rests on the differences one might expect to find between heterosexual and homosexual males. Alexander proposes that homosexuality is somehow a side effect of intense selection for heterosexuality and that masturbation may be a key factor here. At least two hypotheses seem worth checking. First, there seems to be an implication that homosexual males masturbate longer or more frequently or more intensely than do heterosexual males before they have the opportunity of having heterosexual relations. Might one expect to find that if within a certain period after a boy or adolescent starts masturbating he is initiated into heterosexuality, not necessarily actually going as far as intercourse, he will "turn heterosexual," but if there is no such heterosexual contact, he will "turn homosexual." Of course, how long he masturbates before heterosexual contact will be a function of both the age at which the boy starts masturbating and the age at which he first meets girls as girls. Tests certainly seem possible here, among them: Are homosexual males earlier masturbators than heterosexual counterparts? Do males brought up in the fashion of English public school boys, who live until 18 in an all male, antifemale environment, really have greater tendencies toward homosexuality?

Second, given Alexander's suggestion, one might expect some physical differences between homosexual and heterosexual males. For instance, one might expect homosexual males to be able to sustain an erection longer and to have bigger penises. This last point may be particularly relevant, especially if one couples it with the claim that human penis size is key in human sexuality. The fact that human males have much larger penises than other primate males might be a factor in sexual attractiveness. After all, because of their upright stance, humans tend to copulate face to face rather than by the male mounting the female from behind. Face to face, the penis is much more visible to the female. It has also been suggested, by Desmond Morris, that the size of the human penis might be a function of the loss of body hair, something else that makes the penis more obvious (See Wilson, 1975b, p. 554). Since the crux of Alexander's suggestion is that homosexuality is a function of adolescent masturbation, it is easy to see how having a some- what larger penis might lead to an increased "penis fixation." One might think that if very large penises were causing homosexuality, natural selec- tion would quickly step in to control the situation. Recall, however, that in Alexander's hypothesis, the crucial factor must be something which nor- mally helps the individual in the reproductive struggle. It is the "super male" frustrated by lack of heterosexual outlets who seeks satisfaction elsewhere.

It would be very interesting to know how significant a factor penis size really is in sexual attraction. Western males seem to think that a large penis is a desirable attribute. Many Western females must have picked up similar ideas, if only because magazines like *Playgirl*, aimed at women but pro- duced by men, emphasize features prized by men. This, of course, has been going on for some time. Think of *Fanny Hill*, written by a man, where the women remain unmoved by anything less than a maypole. Are women really aroused by large penises, or, more pertinently, are women in pre- literate societies aroused by large penises? Where does this particular attri- bute stand on a list of sexually attractive features?

Another fruitful area of inquiry concerns the question of whether delay of heterosexual relations leads to homosexuality. I know of no firm evi- dence that it does. Being cut off from heterosexual relations in one's adoles- cence can lead to homosexual practices when one is an adolescent—English public schools attest to the fact. Whether prolonged autosexuality causes homosexuality is another matter. However, does the denial of heterosexu- ality, and perhaps the indulgence in homosexuality, during adolescence really increase the chances of adult homosexuality? Do societies that bar adolescent heterosexuality, and perhaps also adolescent homosexuality, produce a higher proportion of homosexual adults than societies that allow or perhaps encourage adolescent heterosexuality? In short, all one can say is that Alexander's suggestion deserves investigation, but that at this point, it remains only a suggestion.[18]

Biological Science, Social Science, and Homosexuality

By this point, my own feelings about the present state of the science must be fairly obvious. I think that the sociobiology of homosexuality is a viable source for scientific hypotheses and well worth investigation; I believe that all who concern themselves with the etiology of homosexuality ought to take sociobiology seriously. As yet, however, the sociobiology of homosexuality lies more in the realm of the hypothetical than the proven.[19] That the genes do play some role in homosexuality seems to be almost certain, that the environment plays some role in homosexuality seems just as certain, but we are still a long way from sorting out the respective components.

What more needs to be said? Perhaps a few words of comfort and encouragement to the social scientists. Social scientists tend to be horrified of and hostile towards biological science. Insecure at the best of times, they spend troubled nights dreaming of the bogey "reductionism," the rape of the social sciences as biologists move into the human domain. Of course, social scientists are not alone in their fear of reductionism. Those same, very arrogant biologists have much the same fears when faced with the physical sciences; "every biologist suffers from physics envy." In fact, social scientists may take comfort from what has happened to biology as a result of the reductionist impact of physics and chemistry. Although in the 1950s, eminent biologists feared that molecular biology spelled their redundancy, precisely because of the coming of the physical sciences, biology flourishes today as never before. Molecular concepts and techniques have opened up whole new areas of discovery and theory in the biological world. As so often happens, the would-be conquerors have been assimilated to the mutual benefit of all.

What about the interaction between the biological and the social sciences? Can we expect to see the same kind of fruitful interaction and melding? My own feeling is that we can and that the sociobiology of homosexuality illustrates this point perfectly. Modern genetic thinking—specifically, genetic thinking about homosexuality—emphasizes that it is not the genes alone that cause physical characteristics, including social behavioral characteristics. Rather, the genes *in conjunction with the environment* cause these characteristics. I believe the second half of this conjunct, the environment, leaves full scope for the legitimate and fruitful working of social science.

Let me illustrate my argument by reference to the causes of homosexuality. At this point, I am not particularly concerned about the absolute truth of the explanations I shall be considering: I use them to make a theoretical point. Doubtless, what I have to say will be generalizable to other situations and to other putative explanations that still await convincing confirmation.

Probably the most famous of all theories of homosexuality is the Freudian explanation for male homosexuality. All young boys are in love with their mothers. If they are to mature into heterosexual adults, at some point in their psychosexual growth they must learn to transfer this love to other females. Some boys, however, find it impossible to break from their mothers; the emotional links are too strong. This may well be a function of the mother being overinvolved and the father being withdrawn or hostile. These boys sense that there is something wrong with this situation: They are caught in an incestuous relationship, and humans have a universal horror of and aversion to incest. Unable to break from their mothers, they transfer their feelings of distaste for an incestuous relationship with a female to the rest of the female sex. Such boys, and when grown, such men, are unable to respond sexually to females and, consequently, direct their sexual affections and behaviors to males. Significantly, homosexual males usually retain a very close bond with their mothers and often have very friendly nonsexual relations with other women, inasmuch as they can be seen as mother figures.

The Freudian explanation is drawn from the social sciences. Now consider an explanation drawn entirely from the biological sciences, namely the sociobiological explanation of homosexual behavior as the result of parental manipulation (where, remember, this need not be conscious manipulation). Are the two explanations rivals, in the sense that one excludes the other? No, rather they complement each other. The biological explanation sets certain parameters and limits, indicating gaps which can then be filled by the psychoanalytic explanation. The biological explanation does not, however, uniquely demand the psychoanalytic explanation. The biological explanation says that parents manipulate their offspring into homosexuality. The psychoanalytic explanation tells how this manipulation takes place, namely, through mothers being overprotective and fathers withdrawn.

Without suggesting a unique relationship between the parental manipulation hypothesis and the Freudian story, and without presupposing the absolute truth of either explanatory account, I would add that the putative facts about parental ages and birth orders of homosexual offspring are highly suggestive. If, indeed, the parents are older and homosexual children tend to be somewhat low on the birth order, as pointed out above, this would fit in well with a parental manipulation explanation. As the parents' family grows, and, coincidentally, the parents grow older, their reproductive strategy may favor an altruistic homosexual offspring over a competing heterosexual child. It is easy to imagine the form their manipulation might take: the father becoming indifferent and the mother becoming overprotective, just what the Freudian account supposes. It is worth emphasizing again that none of this need occur at the level of consciousness.

I suggest, therefore, that social scientists need not fear the coming of sociobiology. Specifically, conventional sexologists need not fear the sociobiology of homosexuality. Rather, the two disciplines can interact fruitfully. This being so, perhaps one final comment of a more philosophical nature may be permitted. Philosophers analyzing scientific change have tended to see it as falling into one of two camps. When a new theory comes along, some believe that the new theory *replaces* the existing theory, in the sense that the new theory proves the old theory wrong. Alternatively, some believe that a new theory absorbs the older theory or *reduces* it to a deductive consequence of the more general newer theory (Hull, 1974; Ruse, 1979).

I suggest that in the interaction between the biological and social sciences, we should look more for a process of reduction than replacement, at least as regards the explanation of human sexuality. Nevertheless, and this may mitigate the grumblings by social scientists that they no more want their work to be called the deductive consequences of biology than to be replaced by it, I would argue that the prospective absorption of social science would be something at once weaker and less threatening than straight deduction. Consider, for a moment, the way in which parental manipulation is supposed to work. As can be seen, although a place is created for the operation of parental manipulation, its exact nature is left blank. One cannot deduce how this parental manipulation will work. In the case of homosexuality, for instance, mothers could just as easily be hostile as loving. In short, rather than the deduction of the theories of social science, what we have is a need for social science to complement biological science and to explain what is going on at the phenotypic level about which the biology is silent. I do not imply that biology is always silent about the phenotypic level, far from it. I mean, rather, that in the human social context, biologists are as yet ignorant of much of the workings at the phenotypic level. Social scientists have worked at this level and, consequently, are already far ahead in a field that biologists would otherwise need to explore all by themselves.

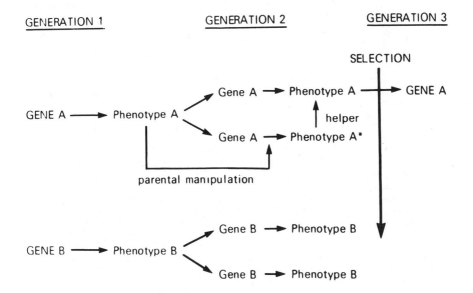

I conclude, therefore, that the causes of homosexuality point to a more subtle relationship between the biological and social sciences than conventional philosophy might lead one to expect. More importantly, the future for both areas of scientific inquiry looks exciting and stimulating as they now begin to work together.

NOTES

1. Actually, once one gets past the title, the article is surprisingly balanced and informative.

2. Full details of the sociobiology controversy and of general claims made by sociobiologists and their critics can be found in Ruse (1977, 1979).

3. As will become clear later, the genes alone do not cause physical characteristics.

4. In this paper, I am not arguing for the elimination of homosexuality, neither am I arguing that heterosexual persons ought to become homosexual. Vasectomies are just as efficient a method of birth control as switches in sexual orientation.

5. I am going to rest with a fairly undefined notion of homosexuality: The homosexual individual is attracted to her/his own sex and most probably has sexual relations with her/his own sex. I would appreciate readers' comments on whether I ought to define homosexuality more carefully, and if I should distinguish the different kinds of homosexuality or homosexual men and women.

6. I trust that I am not prejudging issues by ignoring the fact that one of human sociobiology's most vocal critics, R. C. Lewontin, has argued (1974) that the chromosome is more crucial than the gene.

7. Here, as elsewhere, I do not mean to suggest that genetic sociobiological explanations necessarily imply conscious awareness of one's own optimal evolutionary strategy. Often, even with humans, no awareness is presupposed; it is even denied. The point is that the genes program one to behave *as if* one were aware.

8. Obviously, the relationship is no closer if one has only one child; but in that case, kin selection apart, all of one's reproductive hopes rest on that child.

9. This idea comes in a letter written by Richard Alexander (University of Michigan) to Fred Suppe (University of Maryland), February 13, 1978. In a letter to me, Suppe tells me that he thinks the idea has considerable merit.

10. Of course, the genes are not themselves homosexual. By "homosexual gene" is meant homosexual-orientation-causing gene.

11. I discuss, with references, both conceptual and empirical questions surrounding the genetics of IQ in Ruse (1979).

12. Waddington (1957) discussed this phenomenon extensively in the context of fruit-fly wing deformities. Whether, as he thought, this is the key to an important evolutionary mechanism is a moot point. (See Williams, 1966; and also Ruse, 1973.)

13. Abe and Moran (1969) and Slater (1962). See also Birtchnell (1972), Siegelman (1973), and Weinrich (1976). If any readers have any thoughts on this subject, I would appreciate hearing from them.

14. Indeed, the fact that members of different races have different body sizes has been of great interest to evolutionists. It is the basis of the evolutionary rule, Bergmann's principle, that members of races in colder climates tend to be larger than conspecifies in warmer climates. Various explanations have been sought (Ruse, 1973).

15. A matter on which Weinrich does not speculate is the possible pertinence to his case of a phenomenon in our own society, the Roman Catholic clergy. They have considerable influence, particularly in southern and rural Europe and in South America, and this influence obviously comes from their priestly roles. Is it significant that they abstain from heterosexual relationships and wear clothing which is far closer to that of women than men? It would be interesting to have answers to a number of questions. Does having a priest in the family raise the family's status? Do priests actively aid their siblings and their nephews and nieces? Why do men become priests? Are they often sickly children, are they down the birth order, are their mothers highly

instrumental in their career choices? The one question which will probably never be answered is What connection, if any, is there between the priesthood and homosexuality? Was Voltaire's Jesuit the exception or the rule? Of course, one difference between Catholic priests and homosexual shamans is that priests are not supposed to have any sexual relations, homosexual or heterosexual.

16. I review some of the evidence for this claim in Ruse, 1979.

17. I would especially appreciate comments by readers on this and related points. In skin magazines, one sees pictures of lesbian encounters involving enemas and the like, but presumably, these magazines are directed primarily toward the male market. A survey of homosexual literature designed and read by males and of homosexual literature designed and read by females would be informative here. On this point, the reader might look at Symons, 1979.

18. Evidence from studies by the Kinsey Institute suggests that male homosexuality is more common than lesbianism, having a 3-1 bias, and also that homosexual males tend to be far more promiscuous than lesbians. Both of these facts add to the plausibility of Alexander's hypothesis, but one could really evaluate their full significance only if one had some likely hypothesis about the causes of lesbianism. In many ways, a detailed study of the differences between homosexual females and males would be most valuable in the search for causes.

19. As a race, modern philosophers, as most people in the arts, tend to fear and be hostile towards science. It will therefore come as no surprise that eminent philosophers have already started pontificating on the conceptual impossibility of human sociobiology (e.g., Hampshire, 1978).

REFERENCES

Abe, K., & Moran, P. A. P. Parental age of homosexuals. *British Journal of Psychiatry,* 1969, *115,* 313-317.

Alexander, R. D. The search for an evolutionary philosophy. *Proceedings of the Royal Society of Victoria Australia,* 1971, *84,* 99-120.

Alexander, R. D. The evolution of social behavior. *Annual Review of Ecology and Systematics,* 1974, *5,* 325-384.

Alexander, R. D. The search for a general theory of behavior. *Behavioral Science,* 1975, *20,* 77-100.

Barash, D. P. *Sociobiology and behavior.* New York: Elsevier, 1977.

Birtchnell, J. Birth order and mental illness: A control study. *Social Psychiatry,* 1972, *7,* 167-179.

Dawkins, R. *The selfish gene.* Oxford: Oxford University Press, 1976.

Dobzhansky, T., Ayala, F. J., Stebbins, G. L., & Valentine, D. W. *Evolution.* San Francisco: Freeman, 1977.

Freud, S. *Three essays on the theory of sexuality.* In J. Strachey (Ed.), *Collected works of Freud* (Vol. 7). London: Hogarth, 1953.

Hamilton, W. D. The genetical theory of social behavior. I. *Journal of Theoretical Biology,* 1964, *7,* 1-16. (a)

Hamilton, W. D. The genetical theory of social behavior. II. *Journal of Theoretical Biology,* 1964, *7,* 17-32. (b)

Hampshire, S. The illusion of sociobiology. *New York Review of Books,* October 12, 1978, pp. 64-69.

Heston, L. L., & Shields, J. Homosexuality in twins: A family study and a registry study. *Archives of General Psychiatry,* 1968, *18*(2), 149-160.

Hilton, B., Callahan, D., Harris, M., Condliffe, P., & Berkley, B. *Ethical issues in human genetics.* New York: Plenum, 1973.

Hull, D. L. *Philosophy of biological science.* Englewood Cliffs, NJ: Prentice-Hall, 1974.

Hull, D. L. The trouble with traits. *Theory and Decision,* 1978, forthcoming.

Hutchinson, G. E. A speculative consideration of certain possible forms of sexual selection in man. *American Naturalist,* 1959, *93*(869), 81-91.

Kallmann, F. J. Comparative twin study on the genetic aspects of male homosexuality. *Journal of Nervous and Mental Diseases,* 1952, *115*, 283-293.

Lewontin, R. C. *The genetic basis of evolutionary change.* New York: Columbia University Press, 1974.

Marmor, J. *Sexual inversion: The multiple roots of homosexuality.* New York: Basic Books, 1965.

Morris, S. Darwin and the double standard. *Playboy,* August 1978, p. 108.

Oster, C. F., & Wilson, E. O. *Caste and ecology in the social insects.* Princeton: Princeton University Press, 1978.

Rainer, J. D., Mesnikoff, A., Kolb, L. C., & Carr, A. Homosexuality and heterosexuality in identical twins. *Psychomatic Medicine,* 1960, *22*, 251-258.

Ruse, M. *The philosophy of biology.* London: Hutchinson, 1973.

Ruse, M. Sociobiology: Sound science or muddled metaphysics? In F. Suppe & P. Asquith (Eds.), *PSA 1976* (Vol. 2). Lansing, MI: Philosophy of Science Association.

Ruse, M. *Sociobiology: Sense or Nonsense?* Dordrecht: Reidel, 1979.

Siegelman, M. Birth order and family size of homosexual men and women. *Journal of Consulting and Clinical Psychology,* 1973, *41*, 164.

Slater, E. Birth order and maternal age of homosexuals. *The Lancet,* 1962, *1*, 69-71.

Strickberger, M. W. *Genetics.* New York: Macmillan, 1968.

Symons, D. *The evolution of human sexuality.* New York: Oxford University Press, 1979.

Trivers, R. L. Parent-offspring conflict. *American Zoologist,* 1974, *14*, 249-264.

Trivers, R. L., & Willard, D. E. Natural selection of parental ability to vary the sex ratio of offspring. *Science,* 1973, *179*, 90-92.

Waddington, C. H. *The strategy of the genes.* London: Allen and Unwin, 1957.

Weinrich, J. D. *Human reproductive strategy. I. Environmental predictability and reproductive strategy; effects of social class and race. II. Homosexuality and non-reproduction; some evolutionary models.* Unpublished doctoral dissertation, Harvard University, 1976.

Williams, G. C. *Adaptation and natural selection: A critique of some current evolutionary thought.* Princeton: Princeton University Press, 1966.

Wilson, E. O. Human decency is animal. *The New York Times Magazine,* October 12, 1975, pp. 38-50. (a)

Wilson, E. O. *Sociobiology: The new synthesis.* Cambridge, MA: Belknap, 1975. (b)

Wilson, E. O. *On human nature.* Cambridge, MA: Harvard University Press, 1978.

IS HOMOSEXUALITY
HORMONALLY DETERMINED?

Lynda I. A. Birke, PhD

ABSTRACT. This paper suggest there is insufficient evidence to conclude that homosexuality has endocrine bases. The search for hormonal correlates occurs within a model that views homosexuality as a medical *problem* requiring biological explanations and a program of treatment or prevention. This search is heavily rooted in popular conceptions of gender-appropriate behavior, as well as in naive concepts of the significance of hormonal changes.

Two kinds of hormonal study are considered here. Researchers may either (a) investigate hormone levels in adult populations or (b) investigate hypotheses of behavioral determination by prenatal hormones. Much of the latter information derives from animal studies, commonly on the laboratory rat. This paper questions the validity of assumptions underlying these studies—assumptions about the behavior of the laboratory rat itself and, more importantly, about the legitimacy of this animal as a model for human behavior. It is suggested that, although such hypotheses are naive, their current popularity arises from their potential role in "controlling" homosexuality.

Introduction: The Rise of the Medical Model

Homosexual men and women have long been, and indeed still are, outcasts of society. For centuries, this was officially encouraged by the Christian Church, which tended to equate religious unorthodoxy and sexual misbehavior and to regard homosexual acts as a sin and an abomination, often punishable by torture and death (Bullough, 1974a; Evans, 1978). The dominance of religious orthodoxy began to fail, however, during the 18th century and eventually gave way to a form of medical orthodoxy. Foucault has argued, in his *History of Sexuality* (1979), that views on homosexuality began to change during this period, as a consequence of a dramatic increase in

Based on papers given by the author at the conference of the American Association for the Advancement of Science, Houston, TX, January 1979 and the Symposium on Aspects of Psychosexual Problems, Liverpool, England, April 1979. Much of the work on which this article is based was done while the author was Research Fellow in the History and Social Studies of Science Department, University of Sussex, U.K. The author is very grateful to Professor Noretta Koertge for helpful comments on an earlier draft of this paper. She has also benefited from discussions on the topic with Professor Steven Rose and many feminist friends in Britain and the U.S.A.

discourse concerning sex and sexuality. This was, he argues, "the age of multiplication: a dispersion of sexualities, a strengthening of their disparate forms, a multiple implantation of 'perversions.' Our epoch has initiated sexual heterogeneities" (p. 37). This climate of discourse, then, led to a multiplicity of definitions and categories, including that of "the homosexual." Whereas homosexuality had traditionally been regarded as "a potentiality in all sinful nature, unless severely execrated and judicially punished" (Weeks, 1978), new concepts were emerging of the homosexual as a specific kind of *person* (McIntosh, 1968; Weeks, 1977).

> The nineteenth-century homosexual became a personage, a past, a case-history, and a childhood, in addition to being a type of life, a life-form, and a morphology, with a discrete anatomy and possibly a mysterious physiology.... The sodomite had been a temporary aberration; the homosexual was now a species. (Foucault, 1979, p. 43)

This change was important, as it allowed for the possibility that such a person might be suffering from some kind of pathology susceptible to treatments, a possibility echoed in much medical writing about homosexuality today.

The "multiplication of discourse," referred to by Foucault, filled the pages of medical journals with discussions of many other aspects of nonprocreative sex. Readers were repeatedly warned of the dire consequences of indulging in such practices as homosexuality, masturbation, or even of "excessive" intercourse between husband and wife (Bullough, 1974b). In this sense, homosexual activity was seen as hardly different from other nonprocreative sex. It was all to be avoided and was all likely to lead to insanity or death. Homosexuality, then, became absorbed into a specifically medical and reductionist framework that upheld and reinforced bourgeois morality (Foucault, 1979). This and the emergence of "the homosexual" as a specific pathological entity were significant developments. In the light of these, it is of little surprise that those reformers who, around the turn of the 20th century, tried to increase bourgeois society's acceptance of homosexual men and women should argue that homosexual individuals were biologically determined and could not help their orientation. Such determinism was characteristic, for example, of Havelock Ellis in *Sexual Inversion*. Ellis, writing at the end of the 19th century when the mysterious effects of hormones were beginning to be documented (Borrell, 1976), suggested that such hormones might be a causal factor in the development of the "true invert," i.e., a biologically determined "homosexual." Ellis distinguished these from "perverts," those who indulged in occasional homosexual acts to satisfy lust or curiosity. In this way, the concept of certain kinds of sexual behavior as sinful or wrong was maintained and incorporated into newer concepts. Only the true invert could be equated with emerging ideas of "the homosexual," and only the true invert was fully deserving of pity (Weeks, 1977).

Since that time, a number of theories of the etiology of homosexuality have been proposed within a biological framework. Most, if not all, of these assume that any demonstrable biological differences between heterosexual and homosexual groups represent abnormalities of development. For example, on the basis of their findings that electroencephalograms (EEGs) of homosexual subjects were slightly different from those of a heterosexual sample, Papatheophilou, James, and Orwin (1975) suggest that homosexual men and women suffer from "a degree of cerebral immaturity." Similarly, Griffiths, Merry, Browning, Eisenger, Huntsman, Lord, Polani, Tanner, and Whitehouse (1974) refer to their failure to demonstrate a "consistent pattern of hormonal abnormality."

Many of these theories are based upon a search for hormonal correlates of homosexuality; it is these which will be addressed here. Hormonal hypotheses fall into two types: those implying an abnormality of adult hormonal output (the etiology of which is not always discussed), and those implying an abnormality of sexual differentiation of the brain during prenatal life. In discussing these, it will be necessary to examine the validity of the biological hypotheses themselves, that is, to look at the assumptions, derived from biology, on which these hypotheses rest and to question the methodology employed in many studies of hormones and homosexuality. It is the author's thesis that, on the basis of available evidence, it cannot be concluded that there is any hormonal cause of homosexuality in either women or men and that the often unquestioned assumptions of the medical model are leading researchers to ask questions which are at least irrelevant and at times result in measures designed to "control" homosexuality.[1]

Hormones and Sex Role

It has been emphasized by others (e.g., Shively & De Cecco, 1977) that social sex role, biological sex, gender identity, and sexual orientation are different, and potentially separable, categories, although it is often difficult to define them. Ross, Rogers, and McCullough (1978), for example, point out that not even concepts of biological sex are clear-cut. How, for instance, does one describe someone who is genetically male, but who appears to be female, as is the case with individuals insensitive to androgens? *Gender identity* refers to the "private experience of gender role" (Money & Ehrhardt, 1972, p. 146); that is, the way a person perceives her/himself as female or male. Money and Erhardt's studies, among others, have shown that gender identity is largely a function of sex-of-rearing, rather than of biological variables.[2] *Social sex role* refers to characteristics of individuals that are culturally associated with one or the other sex, characteristics such as physical appearance, mannerisms, personality, and so on (De Cecco, 1979). *Sexual orientation* refers to a person's sexual activity, real or fantasized, with members of the same or the opposite biological sex.

The primary difference between heterosexual and homosexual persons is, of course, that of sexual orientation. People are considered to be homosexual if their primary sexual activity is with a member of the same biological sex. Note that the accepted definition depends on a person's overt sexual activity or lack of it. The cultural stereotype demands a straightforward dichotomy, so that anyone who does not have sexual activity with a member of the opposite sex is branded "queer." Conversely, a person who has fantasies about members of his/her own sex, while continuing to have sex with members of the opposite sex, is considered heterosexual. This dichotomy ignores the many social reasons why a person may avoid a stigmatized behavior, such as overt homosexuality, even while they desire it. In addition, anyone who refuses the advances of the opposite sex, for whatever reason, is commonly labeled homosexual.

The same conceptual dichotomy permeates research into sexual behavior, as pointed out by Ross et al. (1978) who discuss the tendency of society to see "sexual interaction as occurring only between different-sex partners" so that

> if a male wishes to interact sexually with another male, he must think of himself as, or contain attributes of, a female. This, however, is a valid view only if one ignores normal sexual variation (which encompasses sexual acts not inherently reproductive, such as oral sex and foreplay) and sees sex as a solely procreative measure and not as a form of social interaction or a physical extension of an emotional situation. (p. 321)

Similarly, the "feminine" and "masculine" sex roles are commonly conceptualized as mutually exclusive opposites. As a result, an individual who prefers to have sex with members of the same sex and who tends not to adopt an "appropriate" sex role (for example, a lesbian not adopting a "feminine" role) is considered a priori to be adopting the opposite role (to use the same example, it would be assumed that the nonfeminine lesbian is "masculine"). This dichotomy is common and until recently was integrated into psychological research (Bem, 1974; Constantinople, 1973). However, as Ross et al. (1978) stress, when a homosexual man behaves in a "feminine" fashion, or when a heterosexual woman abhors "masculinity" in herself, this is as likely to reflect social stereotyping and expectations, as it is to be a product of some feature of the individual's biology.

It is also noteworthy that in the hormonal literature, a person's sexuality is rarely regarded as a complex product of many interacting factors. Rather, the heterosexual/homosexual dichotomy is retained, and the biologists search for specific hormonal correlates of homosexuality versus heterosexuality. These hormonal correlates are then usually assumed to be significant causal factors in the development of the individual's sexuality (Dewhurst, 1969; Dorner, 1975; Loraine, Adamopoulos, Kirkham, Ismail, & Dove, 1970; Margolese, 1970). Not only are the inaccurate, popular conceptions of homosexuality versus heterosexuality retained in the scientific literature, but many other inadequate terms are commonly employed (Blumstein & Schwartz, 1977; Suppe, 1979). Blumstein and Schwartz (1977) comment on the pitfalls facing the unwary researcher into sexuality:

> The scientific study of human sexuality has not reached a stage of conceptual maturity. . . . It is not difficult to understand why sex research is replete with oversimplifications masquerading as scientific abstractions. By and large, investigators working with sexual data have accepted uncritically the pervasive cultural understandings of sexuality, and have assumed there to be a simple and "correct" conceptual scheme readily modifiable to the requirements of scientific rigor. . . . [E]scaping scientists' borrowed notions of sexuality is difficult indeed, because these lay notions. . . play an important part in shaping the actual sexual data themselves. (pp. 30-31)

For all these reasons, before the hormonal literature can be considered in more detail, it is important to identify some of the premises on which hypotheses concerning the etiology of homosexuality are based. First, there is an underlying assumption, deriving from the simple dichotomy of popular conception, that "homosexuality" and "heterosexuality" are homogeneous, unitary categories and, therefore, simplistic hypotheses about the etiology of homosexuality can justifiably be tested. This assumption can be questioned on a number of levels: (a) "Homosexuality" many mean markedly different things to different individuals; indeed, it is more appropriate to refer instead to "homosexualities" (e.g., Bell & Weinberg, 1978). The fact that heterosexuality and homosexuality represent wide ranges of life-styles and expressions of sexuality must present difficulties for any simple theory of hormonal imbalance. (b) The hypotheses generated by hormonal researchers are almost exclusively concerned with the etiology of homosexuality rather than heterosexuality. The latter is assumed to be "normal" and therefore needs no explanation. To assume this is to accept popular notions of normal sexuality rather than to pursue scientific objectivity. Yet, as Freud (1905) pointed out, a parsimonious theory would need to explain any channeling of the sex drive towards a specific object, be that the same or the opposite sex.

Second, it is assumed that, since the sexual orientation of homosexual people is "deviant," one of their other dichotomous categories—gender identity, social sex role, and so on—must also be deviant and, consequently, there must be some underlying causal factor common to both. Significantly, it is precisely those individuals who appear to be deviant in other categories who are defined by society as "homosexuals." For example, it is the rather masculine-looking woman who is culturally defined as lesbian. It is rarely believed that "feminine" women could be lesbians, or that "masculine" men might prefer other men. It is these cultural stereotypes, however, that provide the model for research into possible biological factors in homosexuality. In hormone research, for instance, the primary model is one of masculine females and feminine males: The consequent hypotheses are that lesbians have an excess of hormones commonly associated with men (androgens) and that gay men will show an androgen deficit.

Third, causality is commonly inferred on the basis of simple correlation (e.g., Dewhurst, 1969; Loraine et al., 1970). If it is found that a particular hormone output of a homosexual population differs from that of a heterosexual group, then it is frequently implied that this difference causes the homosexuality. Margolese (1970, p. 154), for example, claiming that the ratio of two steroids—androsterone and etiocholanolone—differs between the two groups, suggests that a high androsterone level "is the *cause* of a sexual preference for women by either sex" (emphasis added). Such a position ignores the complex interaction among hormone levels and other variables. Testosterone levels, for example, can be depressed as a result of stress (Kreuz, Rose, & Jennings, 1972; Rose, Bourne, & Poe, 1969), are affected by sexual stimulation (Pirke, 1974), and fluctuate diurnally, even during sleep (Evans, McLean, Ismail, & Love, 1971). It also ignores the possibility that interacting sexually with a member of the *opposite* sex may exert an effect on steroid hormone levels. Effects such as these are demonstrable in some species of mammals, e.g., mice (Marsden & Bronson, 1964; Vandenbergh, 1969), and have been implicated in humans (Anonymous, 1970; McClintock, 1971). They should, therefore, be considered in studies of homosexuality. The fact that they are not indicates the extent of the assumptions underlying research into hormonal mechanisms and sexuality.

Hormones and Homosexuality

During the 1940s, shortly after the sex steroids had first been synthesized, many attempts were made to investigate their possible relationship to homosexuality as well as to investigate possible use of hormones in treating homosexuality (Kenyon, 1974). These attempts were doomed to failure, however, and one reviewer was led to conclude that "there is no convincing evidence that human homosexuality is dependent upon hormonal aberrations. The use of sex hormones in the treatment of human homosexuality is mainly disappointing" (Swyer, 1954, p. 377).

Since that time, there have been a few reports of homosexuality being associated with hormonal aberrations in adulthood. Many of these have methodological faults (to be considered below) that make it difficult to draw any inferences from them. Of the studies which are methodologically more sound, the majority either indicate no consistent hormonal difference (e.g., Eisenger et al., 1972; Griffiths et al., 1974) or actually indicate differences in the opposite direction (e.g., Brodie, Gartrell, Doehring, & Rhue, 1974). Since many studies indicating no difference might go unpublished (Lloyd, 1976; Ross et al., 1978), it seems reasonable to conclude that there is no established difference in hormonal output in adults.

Currently, a more prevalent idea is that the effects of prenatal hormones on the developing brain are important in the etiology of homosexuality (e.g., Dewhurst, 1969; Dorner, 1976; McCullough, 1979). This idea was originally proposed in the late 19th century: Karl Ulrichs, himself homosexual, wrote numerous books on the subject during this period and argued that homosexuality was a product of an anomalous development of the embryo, specifically, an aberration in the differentiation of that part of the brain determining the sex drive (Weeks, 1977). Similarly, when the question of legislation against female homosexuality was being discussed by the British Parliament in 1921, lesbians were said to be victims of an "abnormality of the brain" (Weeks, 1977, pp. 126-7).

Prenatal steroids are now known to be crucial for normal sexual differentiation of the external genitalia and brain in mammals. The embryonic testes secrete androgens which enter the cells of the target tissues. The principal androgen, testosterone, is converted intracellularly to oestradiol, which in turn affects gene transcription. It is this process which is responsible for the masculinizing effect of testosterone on the brain, and notably, the hypothalamus, of mammals. (The extensive literature on this complex process is reviewed by Plapinger & McEwan, 1978.)

Over the last four decades, many studies have been made of the role of different steroids in sexual differentiation. Some androgens, such as testosterone, have been found to be particularly effective, while others, such as androsterone, are weaker (Ward, 1972). More recent studies have indicated that masculinization might be separable from defeminization in a mammal (Clemens & Gladue, 1978; Payne, 1979).[3] That there are two processes— masculinization and defeminization—involved in the differentiation of males underscores the point made above: Femaleness and maleness are not mutually exclusive opposites but are best viewed as two separable dimensions.

Most of what has been said about the effects of early hormones on the later developments of sexual behavior has come from studies of rodents, particularly the laboratory rat. In this species, a variety of different steroids have been studied, most of which effectively alter some features of sexual differentiation even if injected in the early neonatal period. In particular, such hormones can affect the normal cyclic responses of a female's brain (Barraclough & Gorski, 1962) and might also influence the development of sexual behavior later in life. For example, when newborn female rats that have been given testosterone grow up, they are more likely than untreated control females to show behavior patterns defined as more characteristic of the male. They tend to mount other individuals more, for instance, and to be less inclined to show passive receptivity (the lordosis posture, normally exhibited by females at the height of oestrus). That in itself is not particularly remarkable. What is interesting, however, is that this tendency to show *male-like* behavior is often termed *homosexual* behavior. The equation between male-like behavior and female homosexuality is widespread in the literature. In a recent paper describing the effects of sex steroids in primates, the author refers to male-like behavior in humans, with the word *lesbianism* in parentheses after it as though the two were synonymous (Herbert, 1978).

Similarly, an equation is often made between male homosexuality and female-like behavior, such as lordosis in the rat. It is interesting that "female-like" often refers to only a limited part of the female repertoire, specifically, lordosis, the passive receptive posture. Yet the sexual behavior of female mammals consists of rather more than simple receptivity to males. Beach (1976) distinguishes three features of female sexual behavior: receptivity, attractivity to the male (which may vary as a function of her hormonal state), and proceptivity, a term used to describe the female's *active* sexual behavior. Beach stresses that the literature describing the sexual behavior of the female rodent has overemphasized her passivity and underrepresented her active behavior, a point which becomes more forceful in the light of recent data indicating that the female rat plays the major part in determining the amount and timing of copulatory events (McClintock & Adler, 1978). Nevertheless, these components of female behavior are ignored, and the passivity of lordosis is sufficient to describe the "female-like" behavior of male rats subjected to hormones in infancy, and it is this which provides the model for homosexuality.

Of course, not all reports of experiments with early hormone effects refer to female-like as equivalent to male homosexuality, but many do (e.g., Dewhurst, 1969; Dorner, 1976). It is worth noting that Dorner, who discusses these studies in depth, refers only to the hormone-treated animals as "homosexual" and not the untreated animals also used in each encounter. This is in accord with the stereotypes of gay men and lesbians in our society. Lesbians are supposed to be "masculine" and assertive, while gay men are supposedly effeminate. Accordingly, it is not the "feminine" female rat showing lordosis to the mounts of the masculinized female who is deemed homosexual, nor is it the masculine male who mounts the artificially feminized male.

Note that what is being measured in such experiments on rodents is a behavioral pattern—lordosis or mounting—that is defined experimentally as being typical of one sex or the other. It is not easy to see how such simple behavioral measures can be extended to the complex sexual repertoire of humans. Dorner (1976) further suggests that among rats, early hormone manipulations can also alter the *frequency* of sexual encounters with individuals of the same genetic sex. Although this phenomenon is not clearly defined in the report, it seems at first sight to support his contention that the early hormonal environment can influence later homosexual development, at least in the laboratory rat. On closer examination, however, it does not. Remember that female rats given androgens as neonates show an increase in mounting behavior as adults. Most rats, with the exception of oestrous females, will normally attempt to repel any efforts to mount them (Barnett, 1963). It would follow that the rats most likely to allow mounting by a hormone-treated female would be other females, themselves receptive. Conversely, males which have been "feminized" as neonates are more likely to show lordosis than other males. Presumably, they are then more likely to be mounted by other males responding to the visual stimulus of the lordosis posture. The experimental procedure, then, has made it more likely that "homosexual encounters" will occur simply because it has altered the probability of occurrence of specific behavioral patterns. The experiment tells us nothing, however, about sexual preference per se.

Further work from Dorner's laboratory had included a study of the "oestrogen feedback" effect in heterosexual and homosexual men, again based on findings from the laboratory rat. The oestrogen feedback effect is most evident in adult females in which high oestrogen levels stimulate a surge of luteinizing hormone (LH) from the anterior pituitary. In the normal female mammal, this is the process whereby ovulation is brought about. The embryonic brain apparently has this female pattern of sensitivity to oestrogen feedback; in males, however, androgens act early in development to switch off the parts of the brain (anterior hypothalamus) responsible for cyclicity (Barraclough & Gorski, 1962). In females, no such switch occurs, and the hypothalamus remains cyclic and capable of triggering a surge of LH in response to high plasma levels of oestrogen.

Dorner's claim is that the oestrogen feedback effect is not seen in normal male rodents, but is demonstrable in "feminized" males. From this, he argues that an oestrogen feedback effect should readily be shown in homosexual men, as a result of insufficient masculinization of the brain during foetal life; and conversely, that it should not readily be shown in lesbians.

This, of course, would fit with the notion that homosexual men are feminine. There are, however, a number of reasons for greeting his claim with skepticism.

First, while no such feedback is readily demonstrable in normal male rodents, it can be demonstrated in adult-castrated male rats (Dorner et al., 1975), and in males of some primate species. For example, among rhesus monkeys and marmosets, there is evidence that raised oestrogen levels can lead to LH surges in males (e.g., Hodges & Hearn, 1978; Karsch, Dierschke, & Knobil, 1973). This would suggest that oestrogen feedback may not be the anomalous effect that Dorner (1976) implies, if species other than rats are considered.

Second, the feedback was only demonstrated in about half of a very small sample (N = 21) of homosexual men, and the surges of LH obtained were rather small (approximately 3 m.I.U.'s: the healthy human female has an LH surge at ovulation of over 100 m.I.U.'s). It is suggested that the small scale of these results might be due to endogenous testosterone which was blocking LH release. No explanation is offered, however, for why this putative blocking effect fails in some individuals: It is clearly not a result of different testosterone levels per se, since Dorner himself admits that these do not differ significantly in heterosexual and homosexual men.

Thirdly, testosterone secretion is by no means a steady state. Since it is possible that sexual activity, or stress, or some other variable, might affect testosterone (and hence LH levels) differently in the two groups, these factors should be taken into consideration in carrying out the experiment. If differences between the two groups are to be reliably associated with sexual orientation, then experimental design must attempt to control for differences in life-style, and for their possible influences on physiological variables. In at least some of the research on oestrogen feedback effects, the gay men used as subjects were attending hospital for treatment of venereal disease (Dorner et al., 1975; Krell, Dorner, Masius, Rohde, & Elste, 1975). This might well impose some stress on the men concerned and thereby alter their hormone levels.

In the light of these objections, it seems premature to claim that a "feminized" brain response can be found in homosexual males. Implicit in these investigations of the oestrogen feedback effect is the idea that effeminacy and a "feminine" brain response are causally linked. Unfortunately for this notion, one of the studies has noted that the effect is more easily demonstrated in those homosexual men who "do not look gay" than in those who were overtly effeminate (Krell et al., 1975).

Methods and Mythology

The generation of hypotheses implying that homosexuality results from an aberration of prenatal steroid secretion locates homosexuality firmly within the "sickness" model referred to at the beginning of this paper and serves to perpetuate popular concepts of gender and sexuality. Moreover, the studies themselves are frequently inadequate, as they are based on very small samples (e.g., Loraine et al., 1970, used four women and three men), and commonly lack suitable controls. Studies of lesbians, for example, may compare a self-selected group (e.g., volunteers from lesbian organizations) with a group of young married women (e.g., Kenyon, 1968) or even young mothers (e.g., Griffiths et al., 1974). Such groups make rather inadequate controls for unmarried lesbian women, most of whom will have no children or may have lost custody of their children. With so many variables uncontrolled, it seems inappropriate to draw conclusions based on simplistic notions of biology. If a group of lesbians were found to differ from a control group on some biological variable, then it might be concluded that their lesbianism had something to do with it. One might equally well conclude that that variable was related to not having children, to having to earn a living, to choosing not to live with men (which, it should be noted, is not necessarily equivalent to lesbianism), or to some other feature of their lifestyle.

Another strange methodological device was employed by Margolese (1970) in his study of the excretion of androgenic metabolites in homosexual men. He used a homosexual sample, a heterosexual sample—and a sample of "unhealthy" heterosexual men. He found that the endocrine state of the homosexual men was most similar to that of the unhealthy heterosexual men. This might indicate a number of things, including that the demonstrated endocrine pattern was a response to stress. Yet Margolese felt able to conclude that that hormone pattern might be causally related to the development of homosexuality.

Finally, few of the papers cited here address the problems of definition. "Homosexual" is a term applied to anyone who has sex with a member of the same biological sex. Thus, some studies include within the homosexual sample individuals who might also be having heterosexual sex (Griffiths et al., 1974, include in their lesbian sample two women who were taking oral contraceptives). Alternatively, the "heterosexual" data may be confounded by including data from bisexual men and women (e.g., Dorner, 1976), or the "homosexual" data conflated by including transsexuals within the homosexual sample (e.g., Meyer-Bahlberg, 1978). There are several reasons why it may be more appropriate to view transsexuals differently from a homosexual population (Ross et al., 1978), not the least of which is that transsexuals commonly seek hormone treatment.

Conclusions

It seems that many of the claims made in the literature on hormones and sexuality are largely based on a set of assumptions and prejudices about what it means to be homosexual, including the notion that to be homosexual is to be abnormal or sick. It is within the sickness model that most hypotheses regarding possible endocrine bases for homosexual development are generated. In particular, current theories emphasize the prenatal hormone environment in the determination of homosexuality.

Studies of the etiology of homosexuality rarely question why the research is done at all. "Homosexuality" is seen as a social problem requiring adequate research to uncover its origins. One consequence of this restrictive viewpoint—whether intended by the individual researchers or not—is that the findings may be used in an attempt to alter those people defined as deviant. This danger is apparent in the writings of at least one researcher. Dorner concludes, on the basis of his extensive studies of the laboratory rat, that it might be possible to "prevent inborn errors of metabolism" (in which he includes homosexuality) by giving pregnant women injections of steroid hormones or their antagonists (Dorner, 1976; 1979). This suggestion is not accompanied by any discussion of possible deleterious effects on the foetus (such as the effects which resulted from the use of stilboestrol to prevent miscarriages: Weiss, 1975), nor of the ethics of such procedures. The possibility of using hormones to prevent homosexuality was also suggested in a popular science program on British television (BBC television, "The Fight to be Male," screened on 21 May 1979).

Dorner (1976) also discusses surgery as a possible treatment for homosexual men and women. Studies of hormone-treated rats have indicated that hypothalamic lesions can reduce their capacity to "behave homosexually" (i.e., to show copulatory postures defined as appropriate to the other sex), from which he concludes: "If our data can be confirmed in other species, a destruction of the "female mating centre" (i.e., the ventromedial hypothalamus). . . could be taken into consideration for homosexual men." (p. 140) At most, such destructive surgery might lower libido (and might well alter physiological functions). Attempts to alter sexual orientation by a variety of means have, however, usually failed (McConaghy, 1976). This is perhaps an extreme example of the forms of social control that can flow from defining homosexuality as a sickness. Rose and Rose (1976) discuss the wider use of neurosurgery as a form of social control, and comment:

> Surgical removal of such brain regions (e.g., the hypothalamus) has been both proposed and practiced to deal with individuals suffering from "behaviour problems" without any obvious "organic" brain dysfunctions. Such psychosurgery is intended as a pacifier, producing better adjusted individuals, easier to maintain in institutions or at home. (p. 104)

Perhaps such brutal treatment is relatively uncommon, but it should be borne in mind that homosexual individuals have often been subjected to brutal treatments, such as aversion therapy (Feldman, 1966). Furthermore, the very process of labeling homosexuals as sick or deviant is in itself a form of social control. Not only does it provide opportunities for a variety of treatments or prophylaxes, but it perpetuates the popular mythology that homosexuality represents a unitary—and abnormal—state.

The medical model, then, arose as "the homosexual" was being defined, and within this model, it has seemed appropriate to ask what the physiological basis of such deviant behavior might be. As suggested above, the objectivity of many investigators should be doubted, despite their presentation in a scientific format within medical journals. More importantly, they maintain a popular set of assumptions about gender and sexuality and thereby serve to perpetuate the view that homosexuality is sick. In this sense, they serve a specifically ideological role.

NOTES

1. Far more research is done on homosexual males than on lesbians. Charlotte Wolff (1971) suggests that the apparent invisibility of lesbians, which is made manifest in the pages of medical journals, is due to men not taking them seriously and seeing lesbians as a joke.

2. This has not, however, prevented Money and his colleagues from suggesting that homosexuality represents an anomaly of gender identity. See Ross et al. (1978) for a critical discussion.

3. Development proceeds according to a female pattern in the absence of androgens in large quantities. However, even in female mammals, some "defeminization" occurs as a result of small amounts of androgens produced by the foetus (Clemens & Gladue, 1978): That is, females given anti-androgen drugs before birth show a greater incidence of "feminine" behaviors than do normal females.

REFERENCES

Anonymous. Effects of sexual activity on beard growth in man. *Nature, London,* 1970, *226,* 869-70.

Barnett, S. A. *A study in behaviour.* London: Methuen, 1963.

Barraclough, C. A., & Gorski, R. A. Studies on mating behaviour in the androgen-sterilised female rat in relation to the hypothalamic regulation of sexual behaviour. *Journal of Endocrinology,* 1962, *25,* 175-182.

Beach, F. A. Sexual attractivity, proceptivity and receptivity in female mammals. *Hormones and Behavior,* 1976, *7,* 105-182.

Bell, A. P., & Weinberg, M. S. *Homosexualities: A study of diversity among men and women.* London: Mitchell Beazley, 1978.

Bem, S. L. The measurement of psychological androgyny. *Journal of Consulting and Clinical Psychology,* 1974, *42,* 155-162.

Blumstein, P. W., & Schwartz, P. Bisexuality: Some social psychological issues. *Journal of Social Issues,* 1977, *33,* 30-39.

Borrell, M. Organotherapy, British physiology, and the discovery of the internal secretions. *Journal of the History of Biology,* 1976, *9,* 235-268.

BBC Television. The fight to be male. Aired 21 May 1979.

Brodie, H. K. H., Gartrell, N., Doering, C., & Rhue, T. Plasma testosterone levels in heterosexual and homosexual men. *American Journal of Psychiatry,* 1974, *131,* 82-3.

Bullough, V. L. Heresy, witchcraft and sexuality. *Journal of Homosexuality,* 1974, *1*(2), 183-2. (a)

Bullough, V. L. Homosexuality and the medical model. *Journal of Homosexuality,* 1974, *1*(1), 99-110. (b)

Clemens, L. G., & Gladue, B. A. Feminine sexual behaviour in rats enhanced by prenatal inhibition of androgen aromatization. *Hormones and Behaviour,* 1978, *11*, 190-201.

Constantinople, A. Masculinity-femininity: An exception to the famous dictum? *Psychological Bulletin,* 1973, *80*, 389-407.

Dewhurst, K. Sexual activity and urinary steroids in man with specific reference to male homosexuality. *British Journal of Psychiatry,* 1969, *115*, 1413-5.

De Cecco, J. *Research in the Center for Homosexual Education, Evaluation and Research on social sex-roles and sexual orientation.* Paper presented at the American Association for the Advancement of Science, Houston, Texas, January, 1979.

Dorner, G., Rohde, W., Stahl, F., Krell, L., & Masius, W. G. A neuroendocrine predisposition for homosexuality in men. *Archives of Sexual Behavior,* 1975, *4*, 1-8.

Dorner, G. *Hormones and brain differentiation.* Amsterdam: Elsevier, 1976.

Dorner, G. Hormones and sexual differentiation of the brain. In *Sex, hormones and behavior.* CIBA Foundation Symposium, 1979, *62*, 81-112.

Eisenger, A. J., et al. Female homosexuality. *Nature, London,* 1972, *238*, 106.

Evans, J. I., McLean, A. W., Ismail, A. A., & Love, D. Concentrations of plasma testosterone in normal men during sleep. *Nature, London,* 1971, *229*, 261-2.

Evans, A. Witchcraft and the gay counterculture. Boston: Fag Rag Books, 1978.

Feldman, M. P. Aversion therapy for sexual deviation: A critical review. *Psychological Bulletin,* 1966, *65*, 65.

Foucault, M. *The history of sexuality: Volume I: An introduction.* London: Allen Lane, 1979.

Freud, S. *Three essays on the theory of sexuality.* London: Pelican Freud Library, 1973. (Originally published in 1905.)

Griffiths, P. D., Merry, J., Browning, M. C. K., Eisenger, A. J., Hunstman, R. G., Lord, E. J. A., Polani, P. E., Tanner, J. M., & Whitehouse, R. H. Homosexual women: An endocrine and psychological study. *Journal of Endocrinology,* 1974, *63*, 549-556.

Herbert, J. Neuro-hormonal integration of sexual behaviour in female primates. In J. B. Hutchinson (Ed.), *Biological determinants of sexual behaviour.* Chichester: Wiley, 1978.

Hodges, J. K., & Hearn, J. P. A positive feedback effect of oestradiol on LH release in the male marmoset monkey, *Callithrix jacchus. Journal of Reproduction and Fertility,* 1978, *52*, 83-6.

Karsch, F. J., Dierschke, D. J., & Knobil, E. Sexual differentiation of pituitary function: Apparent differences between primates and rodents. *Science,* 1973, *179*, 484-6.

Kenyon, F. E. Studies in female homosexuality IV and V. *British Journal of Psychiatry,* 1968, *114*, 1337-1350.

Kenyon, F. E. Female homosexuality—a review. In J. A. Loraine (Ed.), *Understanding homosexuality: Its biological and psychological bases.* Lancaster: Medical and Technical Publishing, 1974.

Krell, L., Dorner, G., Masius, W. G., Rohde, W., & Elste, G. Beziehungen awischen klinischen manifester Homosexualitat und dem oestrogenfeedback Effekt. *Dermatologishe Monatsschrift,* 1975, *161*, 567-572.

Kreuz, L. E., Rose, R. M., & Jennings, J. R. Suppression of plasma testosterone levels and psychological stress. *Archives of General Psychiatry,* 1972, *62*, 479-482.

Lloyd, B. Social responsibility and research on sex differences. In B. Lloyd & J. Archer (Eds.), *Exploring sex differences.* London: Academic Press, 1976.

Loraine, J. A., Adamopoulos, D. A., Kirkham, K. E., Ismail, A., & Dove, G. A. Patterns of hormonal secretion in male and female homosexuals. *Nature, London,* 1970, *234*, 552-4.

Margolese, S. Homosexuality: A new endocrine correlate. *Hormones and Behavior,* 1970, *1*, 151-5.

Marsden, H. J., & Bronson, F. A. Estrus synchrony in mice: Alteration by exposure to male urine. *Science,* 1964, *144*, 1469.

McClintock, M. Menstrual synchrony and suppression. *Nature, London,* 1971, *229*, 244-5.

McClintock, M., & Adler, N. T. The role of the female during copulation in wild and domesticated Norway rats (*Rattus norvegicus*). *Behaviour,* 1978, *68*, 67-96.

McConaghy, N. Is homosexual orientation reversible? *British Journal of Psychiatry,* 1976, *129,* 556-563.

McCulloch, M. *The biological origins of homosexuality in man.* Paper given at the Symposium on Aspects of Psychosexual Problems, Liverpool, England, 1979.

McIntosh, M. The homosexual role. *Social Problems,* 1968, *16,* 182-192.

Meyer-Bahlburg, H. F. L. Sex hormones and female homosexuality: A critical examination. *Archives of Sexual Behavior,* 1978, *8,* 101-119.

Money, J., & Ehrhardt, A. A. *Man and woman; boy and girl: The differentiation and dimorphism of gender identity from conception to maturity.* Baltimore: Johns Hopkins University Press, 1972.

Papatheophilou, R., James, S., & Orwin, A. Electroencephalographic findings in treatment-seeking homosexuals compared with heterosexuals: A comparative study. *British Journal of Psychiatry,* 1975, *127,* 63-6.

Payne, A. P. Neonatal androgen administration and sexual behaviour: Behavioural responses and hormonal responsiveness of female golden hamsters. *Animal Behaviour,* 1979, *27,* 242-250.

Pirke, K. Psychosexual stimulation and plasma testosterone in men. *Archives of Sexual Behavior,* 1974, *3,* 577-584.

Plapinger, L., & McEwan, B. S. "Gonadal steroid-brain interactions in sexual differentiation." In J. B. Hutchison (Ed.), *Biological Determinants of Sexual Behaviour.* John Wiley: Chichester, 1978.

Rose, R. M., Bourne, P., & Poe, R. Androgen responses to stress. *Psychosomatic Medicine,* 1969, *31,* 418-436.

Rose, S., & Rose, H. The politics in neurobiology: Biologism in the service of the state. In H. Rose & S. Rose (Eds.), *The political economy of science.* MacMillan: London, 1976.

Ross, J. W., Rogers, L. J., & McCulloch, H. Stigma, sex and society: A new look at gender differentiation and sexual variation. *Journal of Homosexuality,* 1978, *3,* 315-330.

Shively, M., and De Cecco, J. Components of sexual identity. *Journal of Homosexuality,* 1977, *3,* 41-8.

Suppe, F. *The Bell/Weinberg study and future priorities for research on homosexuality.* Paper given to the American Association for the Advancement of Science meeting, Houston, Texas, January 1979.

Swyer, G. I. Homosexuality: The endocrine aspects. *Practitioner,* 1954, *172,* 374.

Vandenbergh, J. G. Male odour accelerates female maturation in mice. *Endocrinology,* 1979, *84,* 658-660.

Ward, I. L. Prenatal stress feminises and demasculinises the behavior of males. *Science,* 1972, *175,* 82-84.

Weeks, J. *Coming out: Homosexual politics in Britain from the nineteenth century to the present.* London: Quartet Books, 1977.

Weeks, J. *Movements of affirmation: Sexual meanings and homosexual identities.* Paper presented to the Annual Meeting of the British Sociological Association, University of Sussex, 1978.

Weiss, K. Vaginal cancer: An iatrogenic disease. *International Journal of Health Services,* 1975, *5,* 235-252.

Wolff, C. *Love between women.* London: Duckworth, 1971.

DEFINITION AND MEANING OF SEXUAL ORIENTATION

John P. De Cecco, PhD

ABSTRACT. This essay first examines the current discourse on homosexuality and shows how a "gay identity" has been forged within the doctrines and rituals of the gay liberation movement. This substantiation of the gay person is then linked to "the homosexual," created by medicine in the nineteenth century as one piece in a vast mosaic of sexual "perversions." Finally, it is argued that to depict sexuality as fixed, bifurcated states of sexual orientation, and to ignore the fact that erotic preference is labile and interpenetrated by elements of physicality, emotion, and fantasy, is to impede and even to misdirect research.

What's in a name? That which we call a rose
By any other name would smell as sweet.

(Romeo and Juliet, II ii 43-44)

The meaning of sexual orientation has been elaborated most recently by the gay liberation movement, which has developed an image of the "gay person" with a "gay identity" living and prospering in urban enclaves populated by her or his own kind. That this insistence on a new identity is largely in retaliation for the nineteenth-century medicalization of homosexuality is demonstrated by the movement's conception of a "straight" society inhabited by men and women whose sexuality is tightly compressed within the boundaries of heterosexual monogamy, and by the movement's simultaneous invention of a new clinical category, "homophobia," for diagnosing a heterosexual malaise and fearfulness.

Readers who first grant me the indulgence of a rhetorical description of the "truly gay person" will find, in the second part of this essay, my effort to show that the defensive posture of the gay liberation movement, as well as the astonishing alacrity with which society and research have subscribed to its view of sexual orientation, serve only to rigidify notions of sexuality

---

Earlier drafts of this paper were presented at the annual meeting of the American Association for the Advancement of Science, Houston, Texas, January 5, 1979, and at the National Symposium on Homosexuality, sponsored by the American Association of Sex Educators, Counselors, and Therapists, Atlanta, Georgia, January 10, 1980.

51

and reveal little about the corporeal, polymorphous, fluid, and fortuitous aspects of erotic pleasure.

The "Truly Gay Person"

The gay liberation movement has opposed the ossified doctrine that sexual orientation does not exist, i.e., that there is only heterosexuality and the so-called sexual preferences are perversions of Nature, which clearly intended that sex be used for reproduction. This traditional belief is fed by unconscious fears that sexual activity engaged in only for pleasure will spell the doom of humanity. By substituting a single alternative for what was formerly simple inevitability, the movement has imbued the homosexual option with dogma and institutions of its own. A new image of homosexuality has emerged, forged by the tireless efforts of *gay* people writing for magazines, newspapers, and books and meeting in counseling centers, informal rap groups, church meetings, political organizations, and parades. Along with the image, there is a new socialization process, the training required for membership in the gay community. What follows here is, admittedly, a caricature of the *gay person* and of the rituals for transmutation.

To be truly gay one's sexual performance must be unimpeachable, now that the sex manuals (e.g., Silverstein & White, 1977) and the report of Masters and Johnson (1979) have revealed to everyone the consummate skill of homosexual men and women in building crescendoes of sexual ecstasy in their partners. One must start with hugging, caressing, kissing. After reasonable amounts of oral and manual titillation, all systems should go to full alert, and everything that can should become erect—pores, hair, nipples, clitoris, and penis. There are requirements of mutuality. Males are required to insert as well as to be penetrated, to fellate as well as to be fellated; one must swallow the ejaculate. Equality reaches even greater heights among lesbians, who devote the same amount of time to each erogenous zone (breasts, labia, and finally, clitoris) and are equally provider and receiver. Both men and women must prove their homosexuality is no passing fancy. To be truly homosexual one must be pure in thought as well as deed: The male who sodomizes another male while fantasizing he is entering a female, and the female who imagines that it is a pubescent boy rather than her female lover who lies between her thighs, are cheating.

To be truly gay one must have a love relationship with another truly gay person. The unspoken assumption here is that the ultimate proof of one's love of oneself as a gay person is the ability to love someone else who is gay. Such love will prove one is not hopelessly narcissistic (an ancient psychiatric accusation against "homosexuals"). A truly gay male relationship must be *open* rather than *closed*. For lesbians, relationships must be closed, although these now seem to leak a little more air than they once did. The question of *how* open must be addressed. At one point in San Francisco, among gay-liberation males, relationships had to be *wide* open: Partners had to learn to root out bourgeois jealousy when they observed their lover enjoying sex with their best friend.

Relationships are required to be both sexual and affectional and to exist in substance as well as in form. Lovers must build a nest together, live and stay together, share their nest with other couples, pool their material resources, and bequeath what is left to the surviving partner.

One must have gay friends. As one's life becomes wholly gay, only others who are gay can share its joys and sorrows. Holding on to heterosexual friends, especially those of the same sex, is suspect, for doesn't it mean one has failed to assimilate the life of the community, that one's soul is too redolent of heterosexual experience to renounce the past? Coworkers also should be gay. Working for the establishment is aiding the enemy.

The truly gay person must root out internalized homophobia. Tests have been devised to determine how benighted and negative are the individual's beliefs and attitudes about homosexuality and to estimate the degree of discomfort experienced in being close to people who are homosexual (e.g., Hudson & Ricketts, 1980; MacDonald & Games, 1974; San Miguel & Millham, 1976). Although originally believed to beset only heterosexual men and women, homophobia is now known to lurk in the souls of the homosexual as well. By a process of ruthless Augustinian introspection, one must examine one's soul for remnants of guilt, shame, self-hate and fear, and perform the necessary excisions.

Once individuals have forged their gay identity they must return to the "straight world" to explain their long absence from it. No one has identified any single path of disclosure. To be truly gay, however, one should someday tell family, relatives, heterosexual friends, coworkers, fellow professionals or business associates, the community, and the world. Among those to whom one *must* divulge are parents, siblings, and, if they are alive, grandparents. Some individuals first tell the parent they are closer to, others the one they will get the biggest rise out of. Some wait for dessert; others blurt it out in the middle of the lasagna, plunging everyone into silence. Some include aunts and uncles, especially if they were once close. One almost irresistibly discloses to those hated "butch" or "femme" cousins who had barely hid their contempt for one's weird childhood nonconformity. One must come out to old heterosexual admirers, if only to explain why one never capitulated to their lust, and to those one had loved in vain, not only to cauterize shame and frustration but also to show them (with the edge of pride showing like a slip) that one has found greener pastures.

There is no prescribed order for disclosures to employers and coworkers. Individuals who will settle for nothing less than a state of *sanctum sanctorum* start with the president of the university or corporation and work their way down to the secretaries who, they often correctly assume, already know everything. Others begin horizontally with the people in their department and move up the hierarchical ladder. The high-adrenalin types call in the reporters, who then call the president, who then calls the department head, who, in turn, informs the papers that, "Yes, he *did* (I mean d-does) work here."

To be a truly professed gay person, one must do missionary work among the heathen, that is, among the truly heterosexual, those scornful grotesques who still believe that sex is for making babies and who spy enviously through the foliage where gay people romp. One must go to their schools, neighborhoods, and meeting halls to assure them either that we are all alike and should not allow a little thing like recreational sex to keep us apart; or that "heterosexuals" are hopelessly ignorant and prejudiced, fit only to provide gay people with the resources and protection necessary to govern their own, separatist communities.

This image of the gay individual, as a distinct identity, has been promoted by the gay movement in order to win minority status. Once it is recognized that gay people are a distinct class of citizens, it is easier to demonstrate that they are subject to discrimination and, therefore, require equal protection under the law. Several municipalities, in fact, have enacted ordinances protecting individuals from discrimination in employment, housing, and public accommodations on the basis of sexual orientation. Judicial decision is extending this protection to cases involving child custody, the military, and immigration (Knutson, 1980). As an established minority, a group is entitled to a public forum and can summon others to the barricades whenever the establishment gets out of line. When a reactionary faction in California attempted to win voter approval for a referendum which would have banished from the schools teachers who publicly disclosed their homosexuality or those, homosexual or no, who took up cudgels for gay liberation, the model of the truly gay person was successfully invoked by the movement as proof that gay teachers could not possibly convert pupils to homosexuality because sexual orientation, if not ordained at birth, is fully determined in the preschool years.

The Definition of Sexual Orientation

There are many benefits to the heterosexual establishment in recognizing homosexuals as a distinct class. For one thing, recognition protects the class, *heterosexuals*. As Hocquenghem (1978) has written with Gallic puckery: "The homosexual *ought* to be different, otherwise everyone would be homosexual." (p. 107) Also, to think of homosexuals as a homogeneous group makes for easier, albeit much less accurate conversation: It is quicker to say "homosexuals" than to be careful and refer to "homosexual men and women." As people become familiar with the term *homosexual*, they come to believe that there are homosexuals.

This idea of the gay person as a distinct entity was first popularized by the German lawyer, Karl Henrich Ulrichs. His writings influenced the journalist K. M. Benkert (who, under the pseudonym Kertbeny, coined the term *homosexual* in 1869) and Magnus Hirschfeld, the physician and scholar who organized and led the German homosexual rights movement. Between 1864 and 1879, Ulrichs published twelve volumes on the subject of homosexuality, collectively entitled *Researches on the Riddle of Love between Men* (Kennedy, 1980). Ulrichs believed that the homosexual female or male was of a "third sex" (i.e., an *Urningin* or *Urning*). There were subspecies: The "masculine" Urnings, for example, had feminine souls and sex drives but were otherwise entirely masculine; the "feminine" Urnings (i.e., the "queens") were masculine only insofar as they had male bodies. Ulrichs made a distinction between tender and passionate feelings, in modern parlance the difference between mere sexual attraction and falling head-over-heels in love. Bisexual men and women had tender feelings for individuals of the same sex but were passionate only about the opposite sex. There are kernels of truth sprinkled throughout Ulrichs' theory, but we now know that he was confusing social sex–roles and sexual orientation.

Although Ulrichs meant to defend homosexual men and women and spare them blame, he unwittingly participated in the nineteenth-century "medicalization" of sex, an eager identification of new "perversions" which led to a new typology of individuals. Foucault (1978) describes this process of personification for homosexuality:

> The nineteenth-century homosexual became a personage, a past, a case history, and a childhood, in addition to being a type of life, a life form, and a morphology, with an indiscreet anatomy and possibly a mysterious physiology. Nothing that went into this total composition was unaffected by his sexuality. It was everywhere present in him: at the root of all his actions because it was their insidious and indefinitely active principle; written immodestly on his face and body because it was a secret that always gave itself away. It was consubstantial with him, less as a habitual sin than as a singular nature.... Homosexuality appeared as one of the forms of sexuality when it was transformed from the practice of sodomy onto a kind of interior androgyny, a hermaphroditism of the soul. The sodomite had been a temporary aberration; the homosexual was now a species. (p. 43)

Elsewhere, Foucault discusses how society extends its managerial power over sex by implanting "perversions," a task pursued in conjunction with the "perverts," in a spiral of pleasure and power:

...the pleasure that comes of exercising a power that questions, monitors, watches, spies, searches out, palpitates, brings to light; and, on the other hand, the pleasure that kindles at having to evade this power, flee from it, fool it, or travesty it. The power that lets itself be invaded by the pleasure it is pursuing; and opposite it, power asserting itself in the pleasure of showing off, scandalizing, or resisting. Capture and seduction, confrontation, and mutual reinforcement: parents and children, adults and adolescents, educators and students, doctors and patients, the psychiatrist with his hysteric and his perverts, all have played this game continually since the nineteenth century (1978, p. 45)

Both Ulrichs (Kennedy, 1980) and Hirschfeld (Kinsey, Pomeroy, & Martin, 1948) believed that *homosexuals* were relatively rare. So, too, did Kinsey and associates (1948) until they discovered how many males in their sample of 12,000 had had homosexual experiences:

In these terms of physical contact to the point of orgasm, the data... indicate that at least 37 per cent of the male population has some homosexual experience since the beginning of adolescence and old age....This is more than one male in three of the persons that one may meet as he passes along a city street. Among the males who remain unmarried until the age of 35, almost exactly 50 per cent have homosexual experiences between the beginning of adolescence and that age....We ourselves were totally unprepared to find such incidence data when this research was originally undertaken. Over a period of several years we were repeatedly assailed with doubts as to whether we were getting a fair cross section of the total population or whether a selection for cases was biasing the results. It has been our experience, however, that each new group into which we have gone has provided substantially the same data. (pp. 623-624)

If the occurrence of conscious sexual attraction to males is added to the frequency of actual physical contact, the incidence of male homosexuality is even greater (46%). But homosexuality as an exclusive practice is considerably less frequent (Kinsey et al., 1948):

Since only 50% of the male population is exclusively heterosexual throughout its adult life, and since only 4% of the population is exclusively homosexual throughout its life, it appears that nearly half (46%) engages in both heterosexual and homosexual activities, or reacts to persons of both sexes, in the course of their adult lives. (p. 656)

The Kinsey group found the incidence of homosexuality among women to be from one-third to one-half less than that among men (Kinsey, Pomeroy, Martin, & Gebhard, 1953) but more frequently combined with heterosexuality than appearing as an exclusive state. These findings of high proportions of bisexuality in both sexes were based solely on reports of physical sexual activity and attraction. If sexual orientation were viewed as interpersonal and cultural, as well as physical, one might expect that the existence of heterosexuality or homosexuality as a distinct, unitary, frozen state would be even rarer.

To determine the balance of heterosexual to homosexual involvement, Kinsey and associates (1948) developed their heterosexual-homosexual (0-6) rating scale. This was a single continuum, although the individual's assignment to a scale point was based on both physical contact and psychic response to the presence of individuals of the same sex. The "0" classification, for example, indicated that the individual had no physical contact or psychic response to members of the same sex; "6" signified that contact and response were exclusively homosexual. Individuals who rated "3" were equally heterosexual and homosexual. After discovering that homosexual experiences spread across the scale from 1 to 6, Kinsey et al. (1948) noted:

> From all of this, it should be evident that one is not warranted in recognizing merely two types of individuals, heterosexual and homosexual, and that the characterization of the homosexual as a third sex fails to describe any actuality. (p. 647)

Homosexuality, as sexual conduct and desire, therefore, is not limited to a small proportion of individuals but seems to be an integral aspect of human sexuality.

In the Kinsey (1948, 1953) studies, respondents were rated for each period of their sex histories. These multiple ratings revealed that sexual orientation fluctuates, surely over a lifetime and, for some people, as often as the weather. Kinsey and associates (1948) state:

> Some of the males who are involved in one type of relation at one period in their lives, may have only the other type of relation at some later period. There may be considerable fluctuations from time to time. Some males may be involved in both heterosexual and homosexual activities within the same period of time. For instance, there are some who engage in both heterosexual and homosexual activities in the same year, or in the same month or week, or even in the same day. There are not a few individuals who engage in group activities in which they make simultaneous contact with partners of both sexes.

Males do not represent two discrete populations, heterosexual and homosexual. (p. 639)

In showing that sexual orientation is not polarized and immutable, the Kinsey group found empirical support for Freud's argument that human beings have bisexual capacities. Even though Freud (1905) viewed adult homosexuality as arrested development, he believed in the individual's original bisexuality. As a pansexualist, he believed that all human beings are capable of making a homosexual object choice and do, in fact, make one in their unconscious. Blumstein and Schwartz (1977), after studying 156 bisexual men and women, concluded, "Many respondents who had once seemed well along the road to a life of exclusive heterosexuality or of exclusive homosexuality made major changes in sex-object choice" (p. 35). Bell and Weinberg (1978) concluded their study of homosexuality with these words:

> It should be clear by now that we do not do justice to people's sexual orientation when we refer to it by a singular noun. There are "homosexualities" and there are "heterosexualities," each involving a variety of different interrelated dimensions. Before one can say very much about a person on the basis of his or her sexual orientation, one must make a comprehensive appraisal of the relationship among a host of features pertaining to the person's life and decide very little about him or her until a more complete and highly developed picture appears. (p. 329)

The belief that sexual orientation is dichotomous and permanent has carried over to research. Shively and Jones (Note 1), after perusing about 120 studies (most published in the 1970s) in which sexual orientation is a major variable, found that sexual orientation is rarely defined conceptually and in about half the studies defined only operationally. Sexual orientation is frequently assumed, almost always for the "heterosexual" respondents and usually for the "homosexual." The homosexual respondents are often identified by their friendship networks or by the places in which they happen to be found by the research staff, particularly gay organizations and bars. In many cases the interviewer never asks the respondent the simple questions: Are you heterosexual? Are you homosexual? Researchers behave as spies in public rendezvous, who must discuss their mission without naming it.[1] The Kinsey heterosexual-homosexual scale is used in less than 20% of the studies surveyed, usually by the respondent for self-rating but occasionally—and particularly in clinical studies—by the investigator. Even when Kinsey ratings are obtained they are ignored in the data analysis except to classify respondents as "heterosexual" or "homosexual." This was the practice in the studies of Saghir and Robbins (1973), Weinberg and Williams (1974), Bell and Weinberg (1978), and Masters and Johnson (1979).

The Bell and Weinberg (1978) study of homosexuality is more properly the study of the homosexuality of bisexual and exclusively homosexual individuals. Table 1 shows that there were considerable amounts of heterosexuality reported by their respondents: particularly for feelings (44%), less so for behavior (26%).[2] For 33% of the sample there was a discrepancy between feeling and behavior.[3] Further, 71% of their respondents had engaged in heterosexual coitus sometime in the past, suggesting that there is more heterosexuality among predominantly homosexual females and males than homosexuality among predominantly heterosexual individuals.[4] In the Masters and Johnson (1979) study of the sexual patterns of homosexual pairs, even larger proportions of individuals who had had heterosexual experience are found: 77% of the females and the males.[5] Their sample included respondents with ratings from 2 to 6. In fact, 41% of their female and 37% of the male subjects had ratings of 3 or lower: They were at least equally, if not predominantly, heterosexual! After reviewing the major studies appearing in the 1970's, MacDonald (in press) concluded:

> Scientists have confounded their research on homosexuality by including large numbers of bisexuals as homosexuals in their studies. . . . I suggest that it is improper to refer to a married person who has had sexual relations with his/her spouse as homosexual. In some studies of homosexuals the *majority* of the individuals studied may be bisexual. Few investigators think to ask about both the homosexual and heterosexual experiences of the people they study. Fewer still included those statistics in their research reports.

MacDonald recommends the study of "bisexuals" as a class distinct from heterosexuals and homosexuals. Although this distinction would reduce the

TABLE 1

SUMMARY OF BEHAVIOR AND FEELING RATINGS OF RESPONDENTS

(N = 928)

IN STUDY BY BELL AND WEINBERG (1978)

	Behavior	Feelings
Exclusively homosexual (rating of 6)	70% (689)	55% (540)
Not exclusively homosexual (ratings of 5 to 0)	26% (251)	44% (429)
Missing data	4% (38)	1% (9)
TOTALS	100% (928)	100% (928)

confounding he described, it would supplant a dichotomy with a trichotomy. If we are interested in how individuals combine and separate their heterosexuality and homosexuality over a lifetime, the focus of inquiry should be individuals at each point on the Kinsey scales. How does a "Kinsey 3," for example, maintain an equal balance of female and male partners in physical, affectional, and imagined relationships? Do the "Kinsey 0s" or "Kinsey 6s" really exclude members of the same or opposite sex from their lives?

While declaring that homosexuality is multifaceted, investigators at the Institute for Sex Research (Bell & Weinberg, 1978; Kinsey, et al., 1948, 1953; Weinberg & Williams, 1974) have assessed sexual orientation as a unitary phenomenon, as physical behavior and feeling. The original Kinsey group (1948, 1953) recognized that psychic reactions (i.e., physical attraction to desired partners) as well as physical contact and orgasms had to be considered in classifying individuals on the heterosexual-homosexual scale, even though they observed that most of their respondents received parallel ratings. Bell and Weinberg (1978, p. 35) used two Kinsey scales, one for assessing physical contact, the other for sexual feelings, and developed a summary measure of 0 to 12. A respondent was assigned to the homosexual group if her or his score was 4 or more. After identifying the homosexual respondents, however, the authors did not then investigate how the ratings might be related to the variations found in sexual, social, and psychological adjustment.

In order for research on sexual orientation to advance during the 1980s, it will be necessary to study the relationships among emotions, fantasies, and the physical aspects of sex, and to explore how societies and cultures determine which aspects of sexuality are to be suppressed, suffered, or enjoyed. To identify and combine the major strands of experience that comprise sexual orientation, investigators at the Center for Homosexual Education, Evaluation and Research (C.H.E.E.R.) have conceptualized sexual orientation as a distinct component of sexual identity, embracing physical, interpersonal, and intrapsychic factors (Shively & De Cecco, 1977). In this conceptualization there are four components: (1) biological sex, (2) gender identity, (3) social sex-role, and (4) sexual orientation. *Biological sex* designates the sex of the neonate as female or male, a determination usually made by the obstetrician upon delivery of the infant. In most instances the chromosomal sex and the morphological sex are congruent. When they are not, doctors have been known to be mistaken, as in the case of hermaphrodites. *Gender identity* refers to the individual's basic conviction of being female or male. This conviction is not necessarily contingent upon the individual's biological sex. In the case of post-operative transsexuals, gender identity is congruent with morphological but not with chromosomal sex. Gender identity is usually present by the time the child begins to talk. *Social sex-role* identifies the physical and psychological characteristics that are culturally associated with females or males. Social sex-role stereotypes are cultural expectations of appropriate physical and psychological characteristics of females and males. These characteristics are perceived as feminine or masculine. Six aspects of social sex-roles have been identified (Shively, Rudolph, & De Cecco, 1978): physical appearance, personality, mannerisms, speech, interests, and habits. *Sexual orientation* refers to the individual's physical sexual activity with, interpersonal affection for, and erotic fantasies about members of the same or opposite biological sex. *Physical sexual activity* designates the individual's erotic body contact with one or more persons; this may or may not include genital contact. *Interpersonal affection* refers to associations, involving varying degrees of love or trust, with coworkers, friends, lovers, and marital partners. These relationships do not necessarily include or exclude physical sexual activity. *Erotic fantasies* are the individual's mental images of one or more persons engaged in physical sexual activity or involved in idealized affectional (i.e., romantic) relationships.

In the current research at C.H.E.E.R., social sex-role and sexual orientation are conceived along several independent continua. In accord with the work of Bem (1974) and Spence and Helmreich (1978), *social sex-role* is represented as two continua—one for femininity and another for masculinity. Qualitatively, an individual female or male can be seen as feminine, masculine, or both feminine and masculine; quantitatively, femininity and masculinity can range from none to very much. *Sexual orientation* is conceived along three Kinsey continua, one for each of three aspects of sexual orientation. Qualitatively, an individual can be placed on each continuum as heterosexual, homosexual, or both heterosexual and homosexual; quantitatively, the degree of heterosexuality and homosexuality can range from none to very much.

This view of sexual orientation reduces confusion rampant in most lay and clinical discussions of homosexuality, in particular the confounding of social sex-role and sexual orientation. For example, psychoanalytic theory construes male homosexuality as pathology and focuses on the patient's masculinity, presumably underdeveloped and battered by an engulfing mother or a weak, distant, or hostile father (e.g., Bieber, Dain, Dince, Drellich, Grand, Gundlach, Kremer, Rifkin, Wilber, & Bieber, 1962; Hatterer, 1970; Socarides, 1978). The traumatized patient turns to homosexuality to compensate for the loss of masculinity. But what exactly does this homosexuality consist of, and what part does it play in the patient's life? Philosophers of science warn social scientists (and they should include clinicians) about formulating theories of etiology to account for phenomena that were never adequately defined or described in the first place (e.g., Suppe, 1978).

Two sets of basic research questions are raised by the expanded, bipolar conceptualization of sexual identity: (1) What is the relationship of the aspects *within* each component and (2) What is the relationship *between* components. The first set of questions would include the following: (a) What is the biological relationship of being female to being male? Investigation of this question would show what, if anything, is unique to the biological characteristics of each sex and the degree of overlap between the sexes (e.g., Maccoby & Jacklin, 1974). (b) How is the conviction of being female (or male) related to the conviction of not being male (or female)? Investigation of this question would identify any core psychological ingredients, if any, of female and male gender identity (e.g., Green, 1974). (c) How do physical appearance, personality, mannerisms, speech, interests, and habits shape the perception by self and by others of the individual as feminine or masculine? Research would reveal the core ingredients of social sex-role and the relative contribution of each to the perception of the individual's femininity and masculinity. (d) What is the interrelationship of the individual's heterosexual or homosexual physical sexual activity, interpersonal affection, and erotic fantasies? The answer here might identify patterns that typify or transcend the labels of bisexuality, heterosexuality, or homosexuality.

The second set of research questions include: (a) How is being female or male related to being feminine or masculine? (b) What is the relationship of being female or male to being heterosexual or homosexual? (c) How is the conviction of being female or male related to being heterosexual or homosexual, particularly when biological sex and gender identity are incongruent? (d) How is being feminine or masculine connected to being heterosexual or homosexual?

The findings by Shively et al. (1978) provide part of the answer to one question. The appearance of the individual, including body size and structure, grooming, mannerisms, and speech, may be basic to the perception of the individual's femininity or masculinity. When appearance of the female conforms to the feminine stereotype for females, or that of the male to the masculine stereotype for males, then personality can be perceived and identified. When the appearance of the individual departs from these stereotypes and conforms to the feminine stereotype for males or the masculine stereotype for females, the perception of personality may be blocked or blurred. In other words, individuality may be harder to perceive and accept when it lies outside the boundaries of stereotyped appearance. In the early days of the gay liberation movement, some males participated in "gender fuck." With beards, hairy arms, and hairy legs, they would wear dresses, earrings, necklaces, lipstick, and rouge. By combining feminine and masculine attributes, they were able to dramatize the dimorphism of the stereotypes and the ease with which appearance could be altered to cause conflicting perceptions. Both laboratory and field research are needed to determine the relative contribution of each aspect of social sex-role to the perception of the individual as feminine or masculine.

This same study (Shively et al., 1978) shed light on the relationship of social sex-role to sexual orientation. The results indicated that heterosexuality was associated with the stereotypes for feminine females and masculine males, while homosexuality was associated with the stereotypes for feminine males and masculine females, confirming what has been generally known: The heterosexual orientation is often assumed when females fit the stereotype for feminine females, and males that for masculine males; the homosexual orientation is assumed when females fit the stereotype for masculine females and males that of feminine males.

In the absence of research, the relationship among the components of sexual identity can only be assumed. Various aspects of appearance probably serve as erotic stimuli for various forms of physical sexual activity—a particular body build or figure, long or short hair, and disheveled or clean-cut grooming. Particular erotic stimuli provided by appearance and personality may be associated with particular sexual behaviors, such as initiation, following, insertion, and reception. The individual may select one or both biological sexes for physical sexual activity because one or both become generally associated as providers of the desired stimuli and responses. Interpersonal affection, however, may be more strongly correlated with personality than appearance since affection is associated with such attributes as nurturance, dependency and gentleness.

The tripartite division of sexual orientation has been used to pursue particular research questions. In one study (Shively & De Cecco, Note 2), after choosing a label to describe their sexual orientation, respondents (n = 47) were asked to identify the bases of their choice. By far the most frequently (49%) mentioned was physical sexual activity, either as behavior or desire, followed by biological sex (24%), affection (18%), erotic fantasy (6%), social approval (2.5%), and empathy (1.5%). When asked for the specific contribution of each aspect in identifying an individual's sexual orientation, 76% to 92% of the respondents considered physical contact, affection, and fantasy all to be important, indicating that a more analytic depiction of sexual orientation would be useful. In identifying sexual orientation, Saliba (Note 3) also found that respondents assigned physical sexual activity the highest importance, followed by erotic fantasy. In her study, while bisexual and homosexual respondents believed both physical contact and affectional relationships were essential, heterosexual respondents believed physical contact was of greatest importance. Females rated affectional relationships as more important than physical sexual activity or erotic fantasies, while males rated physical contact as most important. Saliba also looked into the characteristics by which respondents designated sexual and affectional partners. As one would expect, sexual partners were described for their physical and sexual attractiveness, affectional partners for their desirable personal and interpersonal characteristics. But there was enough overlap (more for the bisexual and homosexual than the heterosexual respondents) to show that a little personality can sweeten sex and a little sexiness may feed affection.

It is quite possible that for some individuals the various aspects of sexual orientation are sharply divergent, a separation experienced as painful if they seek homogeneity. Masters and Johnson (1979) reported some cases in which male clients presented themselves for conversion therapy, hoping to change their orientation from homosexual to heterosexual. Although entirely functional in their sexual relations with other men, they had affectional ties to wives or girl friends whom they brought along as therapeutic partners. The applicants were trained to sacrifice their homosexuality and to become functional in sexual contact with female partners. Other individuals appear to be able to cross from one sex-object choice to the other without losing a stroke. In C.H.E.E.R.'s study of rape in men's jails (De Cecco & Kellogg, Note 4), the greater proportion of assailants are identified as heterosexual outside of jail while equal proportions of victims are seen as heterosexual or homosexual. What is striking, however, is that "heterosexual" assailants are selecting as victims younger men whom they not only can overpower but also find sexually attractive.

Conclusion

Although the reliability and validity of the findings in these early studies can be questioned, especially because they are for the most part based on small, convenience samples, they do demonstrate that a more analytical view of sexual orientation enables investigators to raise important and interesting questions.

Sexual orientation is one of the few areas of human behavior in which biology is *not* destiny. What the civil rights, the women's, and the gay liberation movements are trying to get across is that "inferiorized" status, signified by race, sex, or sexual orientation, should not spell the limits of individual hope and achievement for a better life and position in society. As scientists, we need to see how viewing sex, qua sex, as entirely physical, except when it occurs within the confines of heterosexual marriage, has narrowed research on human sexuality. Sex is interwoven with our feelings for others, their feelings for us, and the erotic possibilities we fancy in all these relationships.

Sexual orientation, too, is a tapestry far richer and more intricate than we have imagined. When reproduction is no longer the exclusive purpose for sex, is it possible that particular genitalia lose their central importance and the partner's general physical and emotional appeal, the charged situation, and the unusual relationship created within the encounter become the focus of interest? Perhaps Stoller (1979) is right: Our erotic lives are the remains of what we rescued from the pernicious influences that threatened to obliterate all childhood sexuality.[6]

Is it possible to postpone moral judgment, to see that sadomasochism, fetishism, exhibitionism, transvestism, and voyeurism may be playful efforts to dramatize ordinary situations and relationships by giving them erotic meaning? In step with the demedicalization of homosexuality, can we also reclaim from mental illness the remaining "paraphilias"? By recognizing that they are integral to human sexuality, can we move sex out of the prison of domesticity and back into our lives in the myriad forms and expressions that suit individual taste and fancy?

Over 32 years ago, Kinsey and his associates (1948) reminded a recalcitrant humanity about the complexity of nature:

> The world is not divided into sheep and goats. Not all things are black nor all things white. It is a fundamental of taxonomy that nature rarely deals with discrete categories. Only the human mind invents categories and tries to force facts into separated pigeon holes. The living world is a continuum in each and every one of its aspects. The sooner we learn this concerning human sexual behavior the sooner we shall reach a sounder understanding of the realities of sex. (p. 639)

More poetically, in the same vein, Jeffrey Weeks (1978): "Homosexual desire, like heterosexual desire, is an arbitrary division of the flux of desire, an arbitrarily frozen frame in an unbroken polyvocal flux." (p. 21)

NOTES

1. Surely those few investigators who determine sexual orientation in males by clamping a phallometer onto their subjects' penises to detect (gleefully, one imagines) any engorgement that may occur when photographs of nude males are flashed on the screen are viewing sexual orientation as only physical. They never ask their subjects anything about sexual orientation, extracting the "truth" by surveillance.

2. The percentages are based on the data appearing in Table 3.4, Bell and Weinberg, 1978, pp. 286, 289.

3. See Table 3.6, Bell and Weinberg, 1978, p. 290.

4. See Table 3.4, Bell and Weinberg, 1978, p. 286.

5. See Tables 3.3 and 3.8, Masters and Johnson, 1979, pp. 29 & 32.

6. Stoller (1979, p. 31) holds that "sexual excitement is like treading a minefield," that hostility, ranging from mild to intense, is the energy behind it. "We must bear the idea," he states (p. 35), "that sexual pleasure in most people depends on neurotic mechanisms." Whatever the merit of his views, Stoller serves to show how current psychiatric views are still caught up in the pleasure-power spiral described by Foucault. His view of sexual excitement combines the pleasure of delicious, illicit, and forboding arousal with an authoritative pronouncement on its own inescapable, albeit lamentable, link to mental illness.

REFERENCE NOTES

1. Shively, M., & Jones, C. *Measurement and assessment of sexual orientation.* Unpublished paper, Center for Homosexual Education, Evaluation and Research (C.H.E.E.R.), San Francisco State University, 1981.
2. Shively, M., & De Cecco, J. P. *Research on the aspects and dimensions of sexual orientation.* Unpublished paper, Center for Homosexual Education, Evaluation and Research (C.H.E.E.R.), San Francisco State University, 1979.
3. Saliba, P. *Variability in sexual orientation.* Unpublished masters thesis, San Francisco State University, 1980.
4. De Cecco, J. P., & Kellogg, S. *Rape in the county jail.* Book in preparation, 1980.

REFERENCES

Bell, A. P., & Weinberg, M. S. *Homosexualities.* New York: Simon & Schuster, 1978.
Bem, S. L. The measurement of psychological androgyny. *Journal of Consulting and Clinical Psychology,* 1974, *42*(2), 155-162.
Bieber, I., Dain, H. J., Dince, P. R., Drellich, M. G., Grand, H. G., Gundlach, R. H., Kremer, M. W., Rifkin, A. H., Wilber, C. B., & Bieber, T. B. *Homosexuality: A psychoanalytic study.* New York: Basic Books, Inc., 1962.
Blumstein, P. W., & Schwartz, P. Bisexuality: Some social psychological issues. *The Journal of Social Issues,* 1977, *33*, 30-45.
Foucault, M. *The history of sexuality. Volume I: An introduction.* (R. Hurley, trans.) New York: Random House, 1978.
Freud, S. Three essays on the theory of sexuality. In J. Strachey (Ed.), *Standard edition of Freud* (Vol. 7). London: Hogarth Press, 1953. (Originally published, 1905).
Green, R. *Sexual identity conflict in children and adults.* New York: Basic Books, 1974.
Hatterer, L. J. *Changing homosexuality in the male: Treatment for men troubled by homosexuality.* New York: McGraw-Hill, 1970.
Hocquenghem, G. *Homosexual desire.* London: Allison and Bushby Ltd., 1978.
Hudson, W. W., & Ricketts, W. A. A strategy for the measurement of homophobia. *Journal of Homosexuality,* 1980, *5*(4), 357-372.
Kennedy, H. C. The "third sex theory" of Karl Heinrich Ulrichs. *Journal of Homosexuality,* 1981, *6*(1/2), 103-111. Also in R. Peterson & S. Licata (Eds.), In J. P. De Cecco (Ed.), *Research on homosexuality* (Vol. 2). New York: Haworth Press, 1980/81.
Kinsey, A. C., Pomeroy, W. B., & Martin, C. E. *Sexual behavior in the human male.* Philadelphia: W. B. Saunders Co., 1948.
Kinsey, A. C., Pomeroy, W. B., Martin, C. W., & Gebhard, P. H. *Sexual behavior in the human female.* Philadelphia: W. B. Saunders Co., 1953.
Knutson, D. C. (Ed.) Homosexuality and the law. In J. P. De Cecco (Ed.), *Research on homosexuality* (Vol. 1). New York: The Haworth Press, 1980.
Maccoby, E. E., & Jacklin, C. G. *The psychology of sex differences.* Stanford: Stanford University Press, 1974.
MacDonald, A. P. Bisexuality: Some comments on research and theory. *Journal of Homosexuality,* 1981, *6*(3), 21-35.
MacDonald, A. P., & Games, R. G. Some characteristics of those who hold positive and negative attitudes toward homosexuals. *Journal of Homosexuality,* 1974, *1*(1), 9-27.
Masters, W. H., & Johnson, V. E. *Homosexuality in perspective.* Little, Brown and Co., 1979.
Saghir, M. T., & Robbins, E. *Male and female homosexuality.* Baltimore, Williams & Wilkins, 1973.
San Miguel, C. L., & Millham, J. The role of cognitive and situational variables in aggression toward homosexuals. *Journal of Homosexuality,* 1976, *2*(1), 11-28.
Shively, M., & De Cecco, J. P. Components of sexual identity. *Journal of Homosexuality,* 1977, *3*(1), 41-48.

Shively, M., Rudolph, J., & De Cecco, J. P. The identification of the social sex-role stereotypes. *Journal of Homosexuality,* 1978, *3*(3), 225-233.

Silverstein, C., & White, E. *Joy of gay sex.* New York: Crown Publishers, 1977.

Socarides, C. W. *Homosexuality.* New York: Jason Aronson, 1978.

Spence, J. T., & Helmreich, R. L. *Masculinity and femininity: Their psychological dimensions, correlates, and antecedents.* Austin: University of Texas Press, 1978.

Stoller, R. *Sexual excitement: Dynamics of erotic life.* New York: Pantheon Books, 1979.

Suppe, F. The Bell and Weinberg study: Future priorities for research on homosexuality. *Journal of Homosexuality,* 1981, *6*(4), 69-97.

Weeks, J. Preface. In G. Hocquenghem, *Homosexual desire.* London: Allison and Busby Ltd., 1978.

Weinberg, M. S., & Williams, C. J. *Male homosexuals: Their problems and adaptations.* New York: Oxford University Press, 1974.

THE BELL AND WEINBERG STUDY: FUTURE PRIORITIES FOR RESEARCH ON HOMOSEXUALITY

Frederick Suppe, PhD

ABSTRACT. The Bell and Weinberg *Homosexualities* study attempts to subject important prior studies on homosexuality to systematic large-sample retests and also to break new ground in our positive understanding of homosexuality. In this article, defects in prior studies are surveyed, and then the adequacy of Bell and Weinberg's work is subjected to methodological evaluation. Issues discussed include the validity of the MMPI *Mf* scale, questions of sample representativeness, whether "straights" can do adequate research on homosexuality, differences in heterosexual and homosexual sexuality, the role of subculture acculturation in homosexual psychological adjustment, and the use of cluster-analysis to generate typologies of homosexualities.

The focus of this paper is on Bell and Weinberg's *Homosexualities: A Study of Diversity Among Men and Women* (1978). I believe the book is far superior to most previous work in this field yet seriously flawed by its neglect of the complex patterns of socialization that homosexual men and women engage in when they enter the gay community. But the strengths and deficiencies of *Homosexualities* cannot be appreciated in a vacuum. It will be necessary first to examine the substance and methodology of various research studies that preceded and furnish the background for this important book.

Recent Research on Homosexuality

Judged by any reasonable standard for scientific research, much of the sex-research literature is highly defective and its claimed results therefore suspect. This is especially true of reports on homosexuality and other forms of deviant sexual behavior. Experimental bias is rampant: Generalizations

This is a much altered version of an invited paper (Suppe, 1979) presented at the January 1979, meetings of the AAAS in a symposium on "Paradigms and Prejudices in Research on Homosexuality." I am grateful to Margaret Atherton, Arthur W. Burks, J. W. Berry, David Hull, Noretta Koertge, Edward Mascotti, Douglas MacLean, Michael Ruse, Gertrude C. Suppe, Evelyn Young, various of my students, and especially Alan Bell, Pat Califia, and John De Cecco for helpful comments on prior drafts. Martin Weinberg of the Institute for Sex Research has been most cooperative.

are frequently based on inadequate samples, in some cases comprising only one or two persons. For example, Deutsch (1965), Dewhurst (1969), Fromm and Elonen (1951), Hoenig and Torr (1964), Loraine, Ismail, Adamopoulos, and Dove (1970), and Margolese (1970) use samples numbering from one to 13 persons. Samples are often highly distorted, as when generalizations about the inevitable psychological dysfunctionality of homosexuality are based on samples composed exclusively of emotionally disturbed subjects (e.g., Bieber, Dain, Dince, Drellich, Grand, Gundlach, Kremer, Rifkin, Wilber, & Bieber, 1962; and Kaye, Berl, Clare, Eleston, Gershwin, Gershwin, Kogan, Torda, & Wilber, 1967).

Other favorite subject groups are prisoners (e.g., Cubitt & Gendreau, 1972) and military personnel who face discharge for homosexual activity (e.g., Doidge & Holtzman, 1960). Data frequently are highly subjective, filtered through question-begging presuppositions that bias the outcome (e.g., Giannell, 1966; Rubins, 1968; Socarides, 1968; and Henry & Galbraith, 1934, who claim:

> The homosexual female is characterized by firm adipose tissue, deficient fat in the shoulders and abdomen, firm muscles, excess hair on the chest, back and lower extremities, a tendency to masculine distribution of pubic hair, a small uterus, and either over- or under-development of the labia and clitoris. There is also a tendency toward a shorter trunk, a contracted pelvis, under-development of the breasts, excessive hair on the face, and a low pitched voice. [(p. 1265)].

Another biasing tactic is to impose an unrealistic and psychologically loaded classification scheme, force all respondents into one or another "box" in the scheme, and then attempt to draw deep psychological implications about each homosexual "type." For instance, the researcher classifies homosexual males as "insertors" or "insertees," or as "active" or "passive," and then tries to link these divisions with various views on inversion, effeminacy, etc. Studies that employ such classifications include Oliver and Mosher (1968) and Keiser and Schaffer (1949), which classifies adolescent lesbians as "aggressive fighting masculine girls," "outwardly passive girls," and "completely maladjusted girls who had refused the feminine role from infancy on." Control groups are not always used: Using no control group and no test of statistical significance, Lang (1940) studied sex-ratios of half-siblings and noted that homosexual males have an excess of male siblings. Lang concluded that some homosexual subjects are actually "transformed females."

When standard research instruments are used, their known deficiencies often are ignored. For example, although the MMPI is a thoroughly researched and evaluated self-report differential diagnosis instrument for personality assessment, and widely viewed as superior to all other self-report research instruments, a number of its scales (specifically the *Ma, Mf, Sc, Pt,* and *Pa*) are unsatisfactory and their validity suspect (Cronbach, 1960, p. 470). Most of the principal clinical scales have been empirically generated to predict the corresponding clinical diagnosis with a minimum accuracy of 60% (Hathaway & McKinley, 1967, p. 8). Therefore, "the examiner must not evaluate the individual scale in a profile but rather the pattern afforded by the whole group of scales, including validity indicators..." (Hathaway & McKinley, 1967). The preferred research practice is to use one of two standard schemes for coding profiles in conjunction with the many diagnostic predictors for different profile codes found in Dahlstrom, Welsh, and Dahlstrom (1972). Thus Cronbach (1960) is on solid ground when he insists "analysis of MMPI scores, whether impressionistic or actuarial, is at best a source of hypotheses about diagnoses to be checked by other methods.... It is never proper to assume that those earning poor scores on a questionnaire [such as the MMPI] are seriously maladjusted" (pp. 484-485). Nevertheless, a number of MMPI studies claim significantly greater maladjustment for homosexual subjects, even when their means are within the normal range (i.e., below 70), because their mean MMPI scale scores are significantly higher than the means for controls (e.g., Cubitt & Gendreau, 1972; Dean & Richardson, 1964; Doidge & Holtzman, 1960; Manosevitz, 1971; see also the various studies cited on pp. 100-101 and 199-201 of Lester, 1975). Moreover, scores on the suspect *Mf, Pa, Pt,* and *Sc* scales, in addition to other supplementary scales that have failed to gain wide usage, weigh heavily in conclusions of maladjustment. It is inappropriate to base conclusions on uncritical misuse of a single MMPI scale.

The *Mf* scale is abused with especial frequency. Originally introduced as a measure of male heterosexual adjustment, the scale enjoyed such a high false-positive rate that it was reinterpreted as a masculinity/femininity scale. (This may be due in part to the fact that standard procedures for *empirically* generating MMPI scales were not adhered to—see Gonsiorek, 1977). Even this masculinity/femininity interpretation is suspect since the normal group for the scale was not the broad-spectrum sample used for most of the other main MMPI scales. Rather, a separate group of 54 male soldiers and 67 female airline employees was used; the subject group included only 13 homosexual men and women (Dahlstrom et al., 1972). Thus it is not surprising that normalized scores on the *Mf* scale correlate with educational level or that college graduates across the country typically score one to one-half standard deviations above the norm (Goodstein, 1954). The scale presumes that masculinity and femininity are two poles of a single continuum; but factor analysis indicates that the *Mf* scale loads on six different nondemographic factors, only one of which concerns sexual matters. "Masculine interests" and "feminine interests" are separate orthogonal factors

(Graham, Schroeder, & Lilly, 1971). An analysis of Braaten and Darling's (1965) response data indicates that in their samples heterosexual and homosexual males did not differ significantly in feminine interests, but male homosexual subjects had lowered masculine interest scores—specifically, they were less interested in athletics and hunting. Overall the *Mf* scale proves to be completely unreliable as a psychometric measure of masculinity vs. femininity or psychological adjustment of homosexual persons. Nonetheless, numerous studies continue to employ the *Mf* scale and other suspect MMPI scales uncritically, apparently without regard to the validity or reliability of their usage. Similar abuses of other psychometric instruments are commonplace (see Gonsiorek, 1977, chap. 4).

General claims that cannot be squared with or substantiated by the available data are asserted confidently. For example, in a classic study, Bieber et al. (1962) developed a 500-item questionnaire to collect data on 106 homosexual males and 100 comparisons. Statistical analysis of these data consisted of assessing the statistical significance of differences in mean scores on homosexual and control responses to particular questions and of aggregate mean differences on collections of questions summarily combined into a scale. Thus on the basis of statistically significant mean differences on 27 questions (of which only one had a positive sample response over 66%, and only 12 a sample response above 60%), they concluded that 76% of the homosexual sample had mothers who were close-binding intimate (CBI). The researchers characterized these mothers as being extraordinarily intimate with the son; as exerting a binding influence on him through preferential treatment, seductiveness, and inhibiting, over-controlling attitudes; and as frequently expressing pathological sex attitudes and behavior (pp. 46-47). But the researchers' mean-difference statistics are incapable of establishing such a claim about the clustering of these characteristics. Adequate statistical substantiation would require techniques of multivariate analysis; at the very least, correlation coefficients are necessary. Neither of these was used in the study.

One finds throughout the literature quantitative claims unsupported by experimental studies. After frequently reading of findings about the relative strength of female and male sex drives, I became curious how the concept *sex drive* was defined and operationalized. Using the Kinsey Institute catalog of sex-research literature, I tracked down all entries on sex drive and found nowhere a precise definition or operational criterion for measurement, let alone any empirical study of differential sex drive that involved measurement scales. The closest to this was a chapter in *The Encyclopedia of Sexual Behavior* (Ellis & Abarbanal, 1967) which indicated that the notion was not well-defined in the literature and suggested components of an adequate definition of the notion. Conceptual inadequacy is not uncommon in the literature of sex research, as some scientists are acutely aware (Blumstein & Schwartz, 1977). A related problem is the use of the same nomenclature by different researchers to mean quite different things. This is especially true with the related concepts of *homosexuality* and *homosexual*. The variation in conceptualization between various studies makes it extremely difficult to compare claims and results. More importantly, attempts to study, conceptualize, and understand homosexuality on the basis of any one of these definitions can only lead to highly distorted views of homosexual phenomena, a point stressed by Shively and De Cecco (1977).

Given the sorry state of the literature, it is crucial that claims made in influential studies be reevaluated. Alan Bell and Martin Weinberg are acutely aware of methodological inadequacies in much of the research on homosexuality; indeed, they have expressed extremely critical judgments in print (Weinberg & Bell, 1972, pp. x-xiii; Bell, 1975). Beginning in 1967, working with a large sample, they developed a comprehensive study of the development and adult management of homosexuality (Bell & Weinberg, 1978, p. 14). Their *Homosexualities* (1978) is the first of two planned volumes based on this research. The second will be published shortly. A careful examination of their interview schedule for the project (Institute for Sex Research, 1969-1970) makes it abundantly clear that a major motive behind the study was to evaluate thoroughly much of the previously published research on homosexuality. Many questions were clearly aimed at testing individual claims; in particular, many of the works covered in Lester's (1975) survey of the literature are put to the test directly. Because the project attempts such a large-scale evaluation of influential research claims, it is an unusually significant study. Consequently, in the interest of future research, Bell and Weinberg's own study must be examined just as closely. It is my purpose to subject the first published volume of their research findings to a critical methodological evaluation.[1]

The Bell and Weinberg Homosexualities Study

The Sample

In 1970, under Bell and Weinberg's direction, the Institute for Sex Research at Indiana University conducted face-to-face interviews with 979 homosexual subjects in San Francisco (64 black homosexual females, 229 white homosexual females, 111 black homosexual males, and 575 white homosexual males) and a control group of 477 heterosexual respondents (39 black female heterosexuals, 101 white heterosexual females, 53 black heterosexual males, and 284 white heterosexual males). The interview schedule of 528 questions was strongly influenced by a 458-respondent pilot study conceived by Gagnon and Simon and conducted in Chicago. All individuals in the homosexual sample ranked 4 or above on a 13-point scale of sexual orientation summing separate 7-point "Kinsey" scales for behavior and feelings. Ninety percent of the total homosexual sample ranked 10 or above. Of the black lesbians, however, only 77% ranked 10 or above (Bell & Weinberg, 1978, p. 35, note 2). Thus, the study is an investigation of persons whose behavior and feelings are more than incidentally homosexual, the overwhelming proportion being subjects whose feelings and behavior are no more than incidentally heterosexual.

A number of reviews of *Homosexualities* have noted the datedness of the samples, citing the radical changes in the openness and social acceptance of homosexuality since 1970. These reviewers raise serious questions concerning the contemporary relevance of Bell and Weinberg's findings and the portraits of homosexual diversity provided.

Although the reviewers' observations have a certain merit, they ultimately rest on a serious misunderstanding of the incestuous nature of sex research in particular—and of scientific research in general. Credible scientific research is always undertaken relative to a domain of information posing certain problems. Sometimes the problems stem from imperfections in existing theories, sometimes from inadequate data. The domain, the problems it generates, and techniques available strongly condition the sort of research done (Suppe, 1977, pp. 518-565 and 682-704). Sex research is no exception, except perhaps in the extraordinary inadequacy of the research findings that compose its domain. Bell and Weinberg are unusually aware of insufficiencies in much of the research on homosexuality.

As noted above, a specific motivation for Bell and Weinberg's study was to test prior claims in the research literature. Thus, much of their study is necessarily "backward-looking" in focus. To the extent that the study can remove from serious consideration theories about homosexuality which are inadequately supported, the study will contribute substantially to improved understanding of sexual orientation. And to the extent that this knowledge has potential for influencing politicians, clinicians, parents, Ann Landers, social workers, policy makers, clergy, and others, it will make an important contribution to the fair treatment of homosexual men and women. I do not think sample-datedness will seriously affect the book's potential for making such contributions, since the literature and supporting data being evaluated (including those research claims most influential today) tend to be equally dated.

The San Francisco study strives to elucidate the diversity of homosexual life-styles and their correlations with psychological adjustment and various social parameters. Here the datedness of the sample is more of a problem, though not as problematic as some would urge. The more closeted they are, the more the homosexual man or woman's life-style and psychological characteristics will resemble patterns found in the San Francisco study. It is important to stress that the researchers chose a survey site where the gay subculture and heterosexual tolerance had advanced to a level attained only recently, if reached at all, in other portions of the country. Moreover, the sample is diverse and includes a number of the most closeted, unaccepting, and fearful homosexual individuals (e.g., the "dysfunctionals" and "asexuals"). The researchers' goal was not to do a demographic study of homosexual life-styles, but to discern main gross patterns of life-style and correlate them with such factors as psychological adjustment. A case can be made that their sample is indeed adequately diverse, even if it fails to be representative of either the 1970 or the contemporary homosexual population.[2]

"Foreigners" and "Natives"

A far more serious deficiency is Bell and Weinberg's failure to include in the schedule and the data reduction a number of factors crucial to an understanding of the phenomena they investigate. In other cases their choice of factors strikes me as poor. For instance, although their measures of psychological functioning and adjustment were subjected to impressive construct validity tests (Bell, Note 2, pp. 5-6), the authors appear to have omitted crucial factors. These two types of defect seriously affect the validity of their typology of homosexual experiences (pp. 129-138).

These defects stem principally from two sources. First, the type of questions asked and, hence, those factors selected for inclusion in the study, are strongly conditioned by the issues, claims, and concerns of the homosexuality research domain. Quite frankly, such literature is far too concerned with who sticks what, where, when, and how, and with the attempt to draw weighty psychological conclusions from such findings (e.g., the studies surveyed in Lester, 1975, chap. 11). Second, research on homosexuality has tended to have relatively limited input from acculturated homosexual men or women, being instead largely the product of heterosexual professional voyeurs. Thus the questions asked, and the factors selected, often reflect heterosexual stereotyping, experiences, culture, and values. Frequently these have little relevance to typical homosexual experiences. For example, whereas heterosexual partners tend to "make love," homosexual males generally "fuck." Alan Bell (1975) himself is aware of the problem; he writes that it is

> ...imperative that homosexual patterns be related to the cultural milieu in which they occur....Up to now there has been a tendency for researchers to view from too great a distance "the man himself and the world he lives in," to be more adept at data analysis than at acquainting themselves firsthand with the incredible variety of experience and coming up with truly meaningful variables. (p. 426)

The extent to which this is the case is evidenced by the "Ethnography of the Bay Area Homosexual Scene" section of *Homosexualities* (pp. 233-264).

Quite frankly, I found it terribly amusing that the portrait painted resembles so strongly the highly distorted impressions and reactions reported by my heterosexual or just-coming-out gay students after their first several visits to a gay bar, or similar responses from gay students after their first visit to a leather bar. Bell and Weinberg's ethnography lacks the credibility found in, say, Laud Humphrey's *Tearoom Trade* (1970) or even Weinberg and William's (1975) participant-observer study of gay baths.

Bell (1975) continues his discussion of the problem, saying:

> I myself feel terribly remote from those whom I am in the process of studying, writing from lists reporting significant differences between various samples of individuals I have never met and who have lived out their lives in a social setting I have never known. Because of this, and because of a variety of personal and theoretical biases which keep me uninformed, I am convinced that we have failed to tap important dimensions of the homosexual experience. More contact with our subject populations would probably have enhanced my own self-awareness of the diversity of homosexual experience; our study would thus have been at once more objective and comprehensive. (pp. 426-427)

Bell's comments target a serious problem and prompt two comments. First, they reflect the fact that until recently the vast majority of studies of homosexuality were conducted by heterosexual researchers—and primarily by those who were relatively immune from being labeled homosexual simply because they were interested in homosexuality. Thus, one finds psychiatrists, seminary-trained males like Bell, and women, such as Evelyn Hooker, doing the research on male homosexuality. Laud Humphreys did his initial, controversial research on homosexuality as a heterosexually married clergyman. Male homosexual researchers, such as Mark Freedman, focused their research on lesbians. In short, because the socially imposed need to "pass" historically has led to inadequate acculturated homosexual input in the research on homosexuality, the result has been the biases and shortcomings mentioned by Bell. Second, Bell's suggestion that "perhaps it would make sense for prospective investigators to become totally immersed in various gay worlds and in the lives of its different memberships" (1975, p. 426) has merit, but its realization virtually requires that the study of homosexual males be conducted by homosexual males.

Allow me to expand on this. Homosexual people are generally raised to be members of heterosexual society, and their rearing involves the inculcating of values, standards, and expectations of the dominant heterosexual culture. The values, norms, courtship rituals, and social institutions of the male homosexual subculture are radically at odds with those of heterosexual culture. "Coming out" to oneself as a homosexual male usually results in being thrust into the available male homosexual subculture, completely ill-equipped and burdened with inappropriate values and instincts. One must reject the notion that it is "unmanly" to suck cock or get fucked and learn to accept sex as primarily a recreational activity wherein going home with a partner can be as casual and uncommitting as picking up a partner at the tennis court for a few sets. One has to learn to cruise and must realize that if somebody rejects one's cruising attempts this says nothing about one's personal worth or sexual attractiveness. One must recognize that lover relationships are likely to survive only if they are sexually non-exclusive. Typically, the individual experiences an element of "culture shock" followed by a need to acculturate to the new subculture. The reprogramming required for such acculturation is comparable to that of a male transsexual becoming re-socialized as a heterosexual female; or to a light-skinned black person, raised as white, who attempts to enter the black subculture as black. Based on my extensive experience counseling "newly out" and other gay college students, I believe such reacculturation typically takes at least three years, and in a number of cases is never fully accomplished. Even when accultura-tion has taken place—when one has become comfortable belonging to the male gay subculture—the problem persists how to maintain one's individu-ality within that subculture. Hopefully one works out a subcultural adapta-tional pattern that is individualistic yet viable. Just as there are Orthodox, Conservative, and Reformed Jews—all of whom are fundamentally Jews—there is tremendous diversity within the male gay scene and even greater di-versity among the lesbian subculture.

The use of sex as a casual recreational activity is so central to the male homosexual subculture and so at odds with the mores of heterosexual soci-ety that I doubt one can accomplish the needed acculturation without signi-ficant promiscuous male homosexual experience. Because to "go native" in the male homosexual subculture requires a sexual commitment difficult to make unless one has a homosexual orientation, the only researchers likely to pull off "going native" are the "natives" themselves. In the past, social pressures and the professional risk of being "openly gay" have virtually precluded input into research design by well-acculturated, professionally trained homosexual researchers. Perhaps gay liberation has succeeded to a point where this now becomes a realistic possibility.

My contacts with lesbians—ranging from counseling experiences to close friendships and regular involvement in a poker group—have convinced me that male homosexual researchers are at best only slightly better equipped than heterosexual men and women to do unbiased research on lesbianism. Immediately the question arises whether males of any sexual orientation can adequately conduct social science research on women. More generally, an issue which ought to be of particular interest to philosophers of science and to social scientists concerned with methodology is whether researchers can ever perform objective studies that capture the "essence" of cultures, sub-cultures, or "psychologies" to which the researchers are foreign. Far too often researchers studying a foreign subculture invent seemingly objective concepts that are operationally feasible but fail to describe the phenomena they purport to study. This suggests, at the very least, the necessity of accul-turated input into the design of the conceptual apparatus in such a study.

One means of achieving this, of course, is to have professionally compe-tent members of the culture do the research. Another possibility is for for-eign researchers to go native. Far too often, however, the participant-observer reports by a native, or by one who goes native, are suspect in one of four ways: (a) Can a researcher go native enough to understand the expe-riences of the culture under study? Can one throw off the intellectual appa-ratus of one's own culture sufficiently to comprehend the significant experi-ences of members of the foreign subculture? (For an interesting theoretical and philosophical discussion of the problems involved here, see Quine, 1960, chap. 2). (b) If one does succeed in going native to the required de-gree, can one translate the native experiences into the concepts of one's own culture without significant distortions? (A classical instance of this problem is the attempt to make mystical religious experiences comprehensible to those who have not had such experiences. See Stace, 1960, for a particularly acute discussion of the problem as it occurs in this area.) (c) The use of knowledgeable, professionally trained, well-acculturated members of the subculture to design the research raises its own methodological problems. Because such researchers may take for granted the value systems and behav-iors of the studied group, they may be blind or biased when reporting the assumptions and norms of their own culture. (d) On the other hand, the "subjective" accounts of "participant-observer" researchers often seem "soft" to "quantitative" social science researchers and are viewed as sus-pect (perhaps because of concern over biases stemming from problems dis-cussed under (a), (b), or (c) above).

As these are difficult methodological issues and cannot be dealt with adequately in the context of this paper, a few provincial observations will have to suffice for the present. First, problems (a) and (b) are exacerbated to the extent that there is a radical cleavage between the culture of the re-searcher and that of the research subject. In the cases of homosexual fe-males and males, as well as of heterosexual females, such radical cultural cleavage does not exist. These groups do, with considerable frequency, be-come professionally competent members of the heterosexual, male-domi-nated research establishment, thereby evidencing an ability to master and work within the conceptual apparatus of a research culture somewhat for-eign to their more basic selves. Indeed, this is precisely why there is potential for improved research on homosexuality if assisted or conducted by homo-sexual researchers—a fact acknowledged tacitly by some leading heterosexual researchers in the area (see Gengle & Murphy, 1978). In the present context, my point is that female or male homosexual researchers can effectively bridge these cultural gaps in a way that male heterosexual researchers cannot.

There seems to be a fairly straightforward solution to the third and fourth theoretical problems, the "softness" of participant-observer data and possible "native-researcher bias." The biggest problem with "objective" studies of cultures or subcultures by foreign researchers is that their interview schedules or other research apparatus frequently emphasize variables superficial to the phenomena studied and fail to include fundamentally significant variables. Thus, both participant-observer and objective-statistical social science research approaches have their dangers and limitations. An effective resolution is to use participant-observer approaches (whether by natives or foreigners) to determine the relevant variables to be incorporated into more formally objective interview schedules and other research apparatus. This method, at the same time as it increases the likelihood that the research apparatus actually investigates the phenomena it purports to, can provide a reliable data base for evaluating the adequacy of the more subjective participant-observer research reports on the same subject-population. (Unhappily, reports of collaboration between these two methodological approaches are rare in the social science research literature.) With specific reference to the study of male homosexuality, however, I maintain that heterosexual researchers cannot successfully go native and that native input to "objective" research design *must* be provided by professionally competent, acculturated male homosexual researchers. I am convinced the same holds true for studies of lesbians. Nevertheless, concern over problem (c) prompts me to hold out for the combined, collaborative input of professionally competent heterosexual and homosexual researchers.

Finally, it is worth mentioning a compromise source of native input into research design when professional native researchers are unavailable—viz., autobiographies and novels. These can suggest to foreign researchers parameters or variables that ought to be included in interview schedules. It appears that researchers on homosexuality have barely tapped this source of input to research design. For example, the bibliography of Bell and Weinberg (1978) cites fictional or autobiographical work of only one gay author, John Rechy (1963), and gives no indication that literary works played any role in the design of the interview schedule. Granted that much of the gay literature that can lend such input was published since Bell and Weinberg first designed their study, there was a sufficient body of literature available to suggest additional variables and other improvements to their study. For example, there were the various overtly homosexual writings of Camus, Genet, Gide, Hall, Isherwood, Rechy, and Wilde—to say nothing of substantial amounts of homosexual "porn." It is unclear how adequate a sub-

stitute for input by professionally competent homosexual researchers literature provides; but it certainly is better than nothing. (A few studies, e.g.,
Ginsburg, 1967, do use such literary sources in their research designs.)

So far I have argued for the valuable contributions that acculturated
homosexual researchers can make to the empirical study of homosexual
phenomena, but their potential contributions to the study of heterosexuality
should not be ignored. Such researchers usually have experienced a substantial degree of heterosexual acculturation, but their perspective on homosexual society, which is usually characterized by a more accepting attitude
toward sexual diversity and expression, should increase their ability to study
heterosexual phenomena scientifically and without alarm.[3] In this respect it
is worth observing that since heterosexual singles bars are essentially "gay
bars for straights," acculturated homosexual researchers, who are likely to
have had significant experience with gay bars, are especially well-equipped
to understand the rituals of the singles bar.

The Sexuality of Homosexuality

In order to underscore the above themes and suggest priorities for
further research, I wish now to pay detailed attention to several serious deficiencies in, and questionable aspects of, Bell and Weinberg's *Homosexualities* study. In doing so, it is not my intention to undervalue the considerable
merits of their study, which I believe to be an impressive piece of research,
one of the best-conceived and most solid large-sample pieces of research
mounted on the subject of human sexuality in general, and an important
"retest" of prior research on homosexuality. I do argue that there are
serious shortcomings in their attempts to establish positive new insights
about homosexuality.

In a passage cited earlier, Alan Bell (1975, pp. 426-427) expresses fear
that, due to heterosexual biases, his San Francisco study has "failed to tap
important dimensions of the homosexual experience" and thus provides
only a distorted portrait and understanding of homosexuality. His fears are
justified. In critiquing that study I hope to draw attention to some of the
more important missing dimensions.

To begin with a fundamental dimension, I feel the Bell and Weinberg
study displays little understanding of the sexuality in homosexuality. This is
especially evident in the researchers' textual discussion but also appears in
the design of their interview schedule. For example, having found that most
of their male respondents spent at least several hours with their "tricks,"
the authors conclude that "it is apparently incorrect to assume that little
more than sexual contact takes place between pick ups;" rather, such contacts "must often involve friendly, nonsexual kinds of interaction" (p. 80).[4]

If by such friendly, extra-sexual contact one means (as I suspect Bell and Weinberg do) anything more than having a drink before climbing into bed, a brief postorgasmic conversation, sleeping before a second sexual round in the morning, or saying good-bys, then the inference is probably unwarranted for a large proportion of cases. It is highly understandable that heterosexual researchers would make such an error. Kinsey, Pomeroy, and Martin (1948) reported that heterosexual foreplay typically ranges from the mere perfunctory to around 15 minutes, with a few couples extending it to a half-hour or more (p. 573). In a more recent study, Morton Hunt (1974, p. 201) reports that things are largely unchanged except for the fact that blue-collar males have increased the amount of their involvement in foreplay.[5] Most males achieve orgasm within two minutes of commencing coitus, often in 10-20 seconds or less (Kinsey et al., 1948, p. 580). Thus, most heterosexual episodes take 17 minutes or less. The focus is on orgasm, with foreplay viewed primarily as a way to prepare the male and (sometimes) the female for orgasm. Remarks made by Bell and Weinberg (1978) in various places (e.g., pp. 81, 171) indicate they share this orgasmicentric view of sexual activity.

My impression, however, is that a very substantial portion of male homosexual activity is quite different in focus—that pre-orgasmic activity is often quite prolonged, and that sustained arousal is the desideratum. Kinsey and associates (1948, p. 573), noting that before attempting coitus a few heterosexual males extend foreplay to a half-hour, an hour, or even more, remark that: "In such cases the petting becomes the chief source of the satisfaction in the relationship, and the orgasm in which the activity finally culminates becomes significant as the climax, rather than as the whole of the relationship." Kinsey's characterization here seems to me to capture attitudes fairly typical of homosexual males. With allowance for repeated orgasms, it applies to much of lesbian sex as well; indeed, Masters and Johnson (1979) confirm that female and male homosexual lovers do approach sexual congress in this nonorgasmicentric fashion.[6] Many homosexual males deliberately learn how to enjoy fellatio, anal intercourse, etc. without ejaculating so as to prolong sustained arousal. One means for achieving this is to switch techniques before ejaculation occurs. In their discussion of the use of sexual techniques, Bell and Weinberg (1978, pp. 106-111) seem to ignore this possibility. In orgy-room situations at the baths, it is not uncommon for gay men who wish to engage in subsequent activity to break off sexual contact when they find themselves close to climaxing (sometimes explaining, "I'm not ready to come yet"), or faking orgasm while performing anal intercourse. I know of one man who was involved with around 35 partners in one six-hour period, engaging in just about every conceivable sexual technique without ejaculating. Finally he became fatigued and retired to a

corner and masturbated himself in order to have an excuse to end the epi-
sode. He found the entire incident among the most satisfying in his entire
career. In "tricking" situations, it is not uncommon for homosexual males
to spend the overwhelming majority of their waking time together engaged
in sexual activity—contrary to what Bell and Weinberg apparently suppose.
Indeed, for a substantial portion of homosexual males, arousal seems far
more important than ejaculation. I know a number of gay men who do not
view ejaculation as significant to their satisfaction. For example, one questionnaire used by a homosexual referral service asked whether achieving
orgasm was important to the respondent (Townsend, 1972, pp. 287-288). At
the same time I must acknowledge that in many "glory hole," "bushes,"
"back-room," and other "quickie" situations, a speedy impersonal climax
is often sought.

The foregoing observations, based on extensive but impressionistic data,
deserve a more careful, systematic examination. Doing so will involve quite
different interview-schedule questions than Bell's and Weinberg's, which
focus on orgasms and techniques.[7] Only with well-documented, reliable information about the sexual activities enjoyed by the respondents, whether
orgasm was important, and so on, can a clear assessment of homosexual
attitudes and approaches towards sexual activity begin. Even such findings
as these will have to be assessed in light of the respondents' degree of homosexual acculturation. More generally, the situation calls for extensive investigation of female and male homosexual sexuality in terms of psycho-socio-
logical and biological aspects—a point urged by Michael Ruse elsewhere in
this issue of the *Journal*. (For surveys of prior research in this area, see
Lester, 1975; Levine, 1980; Morin, 1976.)

To the extent that such research reveals significant differences between
homosexual females, homosexual males, heterosexual females, and heterosexual males, this should increase understanding both of heterosexuality
and homosexuality. Findings about the degree to which heterosexual and
homosexual members of the same sex are more similar to each other than
are persons of the same sexual orientation but of opposite sexes (as Masters
and Johnson, 1979, claim is the case other than in sexual object choice)
should increase understanding of female/male sexual differences. Relative
to this, a case can be made that heterosexual behavior constitutes a compromise between female and male sexuality. This putative compromise is less
likely to occur among (acculturated) homosexual individuals, and thus, to
the extent that heterosexual and homosexual persons of the same gender are
sexually similar, homosexual individuals provide a "purer" sample of the
uncompromised behavior characteristic of their gender. (See Symons, 1979,
chapter 9, for defense of this general perspective. For a discussion of the
merits of studying homosexuality as a way to discovering gender differences, see Tripp 1975, p. 274.)

Acculturation and Psychological Adjustment

Some of the most important dimensions of the homosexual experience concern coming out. In contemporary parlance the phrase "coming out" encompasses a variety of meanings. First, it refers to the proclamation of one's homosexuality to family, friends, employers, or the public and the attendant refusal to "pass" as heterosexual in these circumstances (see Weinberg & Williams, 1974, chapter 13, for a discussion of passing). This is the sense most closely associated with gay liberation. Second, coming out may refer to the process of becoming reacculturated from the dominant heterosexual culture to the homosexual subculture. Third, the phrase may refer to the process of coming to accept the fact that one is homosexual and that such abusive terms as "faggot," "fairy," "queen," "dyke," etc. apply to oneself. We can refer to these stages respectively as "publicly coming out," "reacculturation," and "coming out to oneself." Since all three are extremely important to the lives of many, if not most, homosexual men and women, it is quite surprising that the Bell and Weinberg study virtually ignores the phenomena—as does virtually all the research literature on homosexuality. Indeed, with rare exceptions (e.g., Lee, 1977), one must turn to more popular gay-oriented publications, such as *The Joy of Gay Sex* (Silverstein & White, 1977, pp. 58-71), *The Joy of Lesbian Sex* (Sisley & Harris, 1977), and *The Gay Mystique* (Fisher, 1972, pp. 22-24) to find even marginally adequate descriptions of "coming out."[8] These works frequently display a better understanding of, and are more informative about, homosexuality than is the research literature.

In *The Gay Mystique*, Peter Fisher (1972) offers the following description of "coming out to oneself":

> The person who thinks that he might be homosexual is not likely to embrace the idea with much joy at first. He knows that society strongly disapproves of homosexuals, he may have guilt feelings himself, and he can assume that life is likely to be more difficult as a homosexual. . . . Even if he has an overwhelming preference for homosexual relations and has had extensive homosexual experience, he may hold back from the final admission to himself that he is a homosexual. He may view his behavior as part of a phase that will someday come to an end, or he may feel that with a great deal of self-control and determination he can develop the heterosexual interest that he presently lacks. Many homosexuals go through an enormous inner struggle before finally accepting a homosexual identity and life-style. . . .
>
> In most cases, coming out is a long, slow process that begins with the first awareness of homosexual interests and feelings of attraction for members of the same sex. . . . Coming out is no easy thing. . . .

The act of identifying and accepting oneself as a homosexual marks a major turning point in so many lives. The inner conflict is over and one is suddenly free to be himself. There may be many difficulties in living life as a homosexual....More important, one is no longer at war with himself. The energy which was devoted to denying one's self can now be redirected toward building a happy life (pp. 23-24).

The next step towards building that happy life is the reacculturation process described earlier, the process of becoming socialized into the gay subculture with attendant alterations in internalized values, sexual and otherwise. By failing in their present volume to take into account the process of "coming out to oneself" and all the phenomena associated with reacculturation, Bell and Weinberg ignore variables crucial to an adequate investigation and comprehension of psychological adjustment by homosexual persons.

This is not to say, however, that their interview schedule does not contain questions germane to assessing these dimensions. They did ask respondents to discuss their perceptions of feeling different from their peers, their own and others' labeling of them as "homosexual," and affiliations with others who had similarly defined themselves. The researchers' findings on these aspects of managing homosexual careers will be covered in the second volume resulting from their study (Bell et al., Note 1). Already Bell has written (Note 2):

There is no question but that we might well have done a better job of examining the process of self-definition and of coping mechanisms employed by homosexuals actively engaged in coming to terms with themselves and with the surrounding culture. This is an area of homosexual research which, like so many others (even those examined in greater detail within the context of our study), calls for an extensive inquiry....If we had it to do over again, I would be interested in knowing the timing and the motivations of our respondents' self revelation as well as the interpersonal and/or social circumstances involved. I would think that our respondents' attitudes toward homosexuality in themselves and others also has a bearing upon what Suppe has referred to as the coming-out phenomenon, and here we find the Asexuals and Dysfunctionals more likely to experience their homosexuality as ego-alien than do the much better adjusted groups (pp. 11-12).

This passage (written in response to Suppe, Note 4) acknowledges the fact that coming out is an important dimension of homosexuality which research must take into account in assessing the psychological adjustment of homosexual individuals, and that Bell and Weinberg were not totally oblivious to it in designing their San Francisco study (e.g., questions 393-398, 420-426, 453-459, in Institute for Sex-Research, 1969-1970). From Fisher's discussion of "coming out to oneself," it should be clear that the process often involves considerable psychological trauma and unhappiness but that admission of one's homosexuality to oneself and successful reacculturation to the gay subculture usually insure a marked improvement in one's happiness and psychological well-being. Where one is in the process of coming out and how well one is acculturated to the gay subculture should correlate significantly with other dimensions of psychological adjustment. Thus, any investigation which ignores these dimensions, as does the Bell and Weinberg study, is likely to be highly deficient.

This point is sufficiently important to warrant further discussion. The psychotherapist Carl Rogers has noted that a person's self-image frequently is distorted by various facades, socially approved images, pretenses, and armor-plated defense mechanisms fostered by what a partner says, parents decide, churches rule, schools evaluate, and society dictates as praiseworthy (Rogers, 1972, pp. 207-208; also Rogers, 1961, especially chapter 6)—a portrait, I would add, that accurately describes a person of homosexual orientation who has yet to come out to himself/herself. The dropping of such masks, in order to arrive at an accurate self-assessment, is an important dimension in psychological adjustment. But when the true self is socially deviant, when one discovers and admits to oneself that one is "different," one runs the risk of alienation—and this can be as psychologically debilitating as is any mask or facade.[9] In an ideal world everyone would achieve self-actualization, and this would serve as an important indicator of psychological adjustment. In practice, it is often very difficult to distinguish self-actualization from "mindless conformity" to a deviant subculture's values. For example, are "Castro clones" "self-actualizing" individuals or mindless conformists to norms of the San Francisco gay subculture? Do they enjoy "autonomy of self-worth"—or are they psychological parasites?

At issue is how to develop a strategy for escaping alienation. Superior autonomy of self-worth is the approach preferred by many psychotherapists so long as the autonomous path is relatively conformist. But in order to retain a viable self-worth, those who have adopted a deviant life-style must do one of two things: (1) One must be sufficiently autonomous to withstand charges by unduly restrictive, normatively inclined psychotherapists that one's life-style is pathological (see Broverman, Broverman, Clarkson, Rosenkranz, & Vogel, 1970, which reveals the extent to which professional judgments of mental health practitioners reflect and parallel conformity to sex-role stereotypes; also Hoffman, 1968, chapter 9; and Suppe, Note 5.) (2) Alternately, one can join a subculture of fellow "deviants" and reacculturate oneself to the norms of that "deviant subculture." This provides subcultural reinforcement of one's behavior which can substitute for the sorts of autonomous self-worth evaluation that Rogers stresses as crucial to increased psychological adjustment, heightened indeed to a level enjoyed by few "normal humans" (Rogers, 1961, pp. 119-122). Put differently, it is crucial that homosexual men and women who have "come out to themselves" but who have developed only a limited autonomous sense of self-worth acculturate themselves to the gay subculture. Consequently, to ignore factors of acculturation is a serious defect in Bell's and Weinberg's investigation of the psychological functioning of homosexual men and women. As we will see below, neglecting these dimensions of self-worth seriously mars their attempt to provide a typology of homosexualities.

A final word needs to be said with regard to the adequacy of the various psychometric measures used by Bell and Weinberg. Rather than using standard (and frequently suspect) psychometric scales intact when measuring respondents' feeling states, they combined items from the MMPI, Bradburn's and Caplovitz's (1965) measures of happiness, and Rosenberg's (1965) measures of self-esteem. The initially culled items were subjected to factor analysis, which indicated that five distinct factors were being tapped. The items were combined or excluded in order to raise their loadings and, in some instances, combined or excluded in order to raise their test-retest reliabilities to acceptable levels (Bell, Note 2, pp. 5-6). The missing reacculturation and "coming out" dimensions strike me as being the only obvious defect in their psychometric measures.

The Typology

Bell and Weinberg tell us that "the *raison d'etre* of our study...[is] that we do not do justice to people's sexual orientation when we refer to it by a singular noun. There are 'homosexualities' and there are 'heterosexualities,' each involving a variety of different interrelated dimensions" (p. 219). To that end they employ multivariate factor and cluster analyses to generate a typology of homosexual experience and then attempt to correlate dimensions of social and psychological adjustment with the various types delineated (pp. 129-216). Pointing out the merits of this approach, they claim, "If we had not done this...we would have been forced to conclude that homosexual adults in general tend to be less well adjusted psychologically than heterosexual men and women." In fact, only two of the groups in their typology emerged as more poorly adjusted psychologically than their heterosexual control group (pp. 215-216). Bell's and Weinberg's point is well-taken. Although their typology is defective in several ways and consequently their findings are not as reliable as one would wish, their attempt marks a significant advance for sampling research on homosexuality and ought to be applauded.

Unfortunately, Bell and Weinberg did not develop a comparable typology for their heterosexual control group. In their attempt to correlate psychological and social adjustment with various types of homosexual life-styles, it would have helped if their heterosexual control group had produced a relatable typology that afforded comparable heterosexual vs. homosexual typological comparisons. This could have provided deeper understanding of differences and similarities in heterosexual and homosexual patterns of psychological adjustment. While suitably matched controls for such a comparative typological study probably could be obtained today, I suspect that the paucity of heterosexual experimentation with alternative sexual life-styles at the time of their study virtually precluded such a research option. For example, the singles bar scene (itself imitative of a homosexual life-style) did not then exist. Consequently, the authors are not to be seriously faulted for this omission from their study.

Bell's and Weinberg's typology identifies the following five groups:

—*Closed coupled:* Living with a same-sex partner in a quasi-marriage ("coupled"); low scores on numbers of sexual problems, number of sexual partners, and amount of cruising.
—*Open-coupled:* Living with a same-sex partner in a "marital" relationship; high scores on *one or more* of the following: number of sexual partners, number of sexual problems, and amount of cruising.
—*Functional:* Not coupled; high scores on number of sexual partners and level of sexual activity; and low scores on regret of their homosexuality and number of sexual problems.
—*Dysfunctional:* Not coupled; high score on *either* number of partners *or* level of sexual activity, and high scores on number of sexual problems and regret over their homosexuality.
—*Asexual*: Not coupled; low scores on level of sexual activity, number of partners, and amount of cruising (paraphrased from pp. 132-134).

The same typology was used for both homosexual males and lesbians. Membership criteria were determined by separate cluster analyses for each group.

Before we can evaluate the adequacy of this typology, we need to discuss the procedure employed to generate it. First, multivariate factor analysis was used heuristically to suggest the principal ways in which homosexual experiences differed (Bell, Note 2, p. 13). An orthogonal 4-factor structure was obtained; this is reported in Tables 13.3 and 13.4 of the book. The researchers then analyzed the loadings in this factor analysis and picked 13 criterion variables to which a hierarchical agglomerative clustering algorithm was applied. For this, Bell and Weinberg follow the general cluster procedure of Ward (1963), apparently using the distance function of Veldman (1967, pp. 308-317). Further subjective analysis of the output of the clustering algorithm led to the membership criteria mentioned above. Approximately a quarter of their subjects were precluded from assignment under the final criteria (p. 267).

Clustering algorithms work as follows: Each criterion variable is assigned a weight, and some "objective function" of these weighted variables is used to specify a measure of the similarity to, or distance between, individuals or collections of individuals in the population. The weights assigned may be equal, as in this case (p. 265). Given a subject population of *n* individuals, the algorithm initially assigns each individual to a distinct *taxon* (group). At this point, the distance measure determines which two taxa possess members who are most similar and combines these two classes—yielding *n*-1 taxa. The procedure is then duplicated, the first iteration producing *n*-2 taxa, the second *n*-3 taxa, etc., until only one or two taxa remain. (Bell and Weinberg stopped at two; p. 265). The printout of the algorithm produces as many different *candidate taxonomies* as there were iterations of the algorithm: an *n* taxa taxonomy, an *n*-1 taxa taxonomy, an *n*-2 taxa taxonomy, etc. Some of these candidate taxonomies will be highly arbitrary, whereas others might plausibly be construed as "natural," reflecting *real* divisions in nature. The researcher confronted with this plethora of candidate taxonomies must then attempt to evaluate their scientific interpretation, hopefully finding one which is "natural"—and more natural than any of the other candidates. Such evaluation is very much like deciding how many factors to use in a factor analysis (see Graham et al., 1971)—the researcher must attempt to interpret each candidate taxonomy in psychological, sociological, or other appropriate scientific terms, testing to see which candidate taxonomies admit of a plausible scientific interpretation (i.e., explore the relative construct validity of the candidate taxonomies).

The objectivity of classification or taxonomic schemes generated by cluster analysis generally is suspect. The grouping of individuals into taxa is heavily influenced by the variance *pattern* of the sample population, making it extremely difficult to replicate results with different sample populations. Results are strongly influenced by the choice of weightings for criterion variables and by the choice of distance or similarity measures. (See Sokal & Sneath, 1963, pp. 125-168 and chapter 7, for discussion of the unresolved conflicts over these options.) A further problem involves the decision as to which candidate taxonomy is most "natural." Several decades of experience in numerical biological taxonomy have revealed that experts experience difficulty in replicating each other's choices using the same sample population. There is no reason to think that social scientists will do any better. (See Suppe, 1974, for further discussions of issues pertaining to the notion of "natural" taxonomies and the objectivity of numerical taxonomic methods in biology.)

Fortunately, Bell and Weinberg have minimalized the effects of such cluster-analysis defects by using the cluster analysis only as a heuristic, penultimate step in the generation of their typology. Noting that it is a very subjective technique, they ran the cluster analysis several times using random subgroups of the population with minor variations. They then evaluated the resulting multiple sets of candidate taxonomies against response patterns to determine the most natural taxonomy—one with five clusters. Having evaluated the results of several outputs of the cluster analysis on different subpopulations, they determined that only 6 of the 13 criterion variables distinguished the selected five taxa typologies. Then they repeated the cluster analysis using only these six variables and learned that "in general, the same groups emerged as they did when all thirteen variables were included but this time the groups were more sharply defined" (p. 266). This convinced them that the five types used were satisfactory and that "the labels for each type had empirical as well as theoretical meaning" (p. 266). However, Bell and Weinberg were not always completely satisfied, as some assignments of respondents to groups seemed artificial. Consequently, they "decided to invoke theoretical considerations in assigning members to types" (p. 266) and formulated the rules for group membership paraphrased above. This excluded approximately a quarter of their respondents from any of the types (pp. 266-267).

Collectively, these strategies avoid many of the replicability and objectivity problems endemic to taxonomies generated by cluster analysis. But they do not eliminate them all. Just as researchers differ as to which candidate taxonomy is most natural, similar difficulties arise in getting different researchers to agree as to which individuals are artificially included in a type.

It is my contention that the rules for including individuals in the open-coupled (hence, too, the closed-coupled) and possibly in the dysfunctional categories are seriously deficient in that they artificially combine quite distinct objective or "natural" types of homosexualities. One of the membership variables for both open-coupled and dysfunctional group membership is a disjunction of high scores on one or more of several distinct variables. For open-coupleds these are (a) "number of sexual partners," (b) "number of sexual problems," and (c) "amount of cruising." While (a) and (c) have a significant correlation coefficient (58), neither (a) and (b) nor (b) and (c) are significantly correlated (they have correlation coefficients of -02 and 05 respectively). Moreover, (a) and (c) load on one factor in the "four-factor-orthogonal structure" resulting from their factor analysis whereas (b) loads on a different factor.[10]

It is unclear to what degree the inclusion of a disjunctive parameter in the dysfunctional characterization poses a problem. While the two disjuncts are only modestly correlated (coefficient 45) for males, both disjuncts do load strongly ($-.703$ and $-.716$) on the same factor, and so a case could be made for the legitimacy of disjunctively lumping them together. But when some of the disjuncts load on different factors (as they do for the open-coupleds), their use is suspect in an attempt to devise a typology for investigating the correlation of different patterns of homosexuality with various dimensions of social and psychological adjustment.

There are, I believe, independent reasons for questioning the adequacy of Bell's and Weinberg's open- and closed-coupled taxa. Based on counseling and other experiences, I find that sexual nonexclusivity tends to be a primary factor in the breakup of male/male lover relationships. At the same time, the ability to work out acceptable ground rules for nonexclusivity is the sine qua non of most stable, long-lasting male/male couples. (The reverse appears to be the case in the majority of lesbian lover relationships.) I have observed the way sexual exclusivity or nonexclusivity is handled in approximately 200 male/male lover relationships lasting three and a half years or more. Only two of these couples do not operate under *openly* nonexclusive sexual ground rules—and one of these is a 17-year relationship just now confronting the covert but ongoing nonexclusivities of the partners. [11] The ground rules for open nonexclusivity tend to vary from allowing live-in secondary lovers to "only when out of town," "only at the baths when we go together," "only if you don't bring them home," "only on a specified night of the week," "not in our bed," "no repeats with the same trick," "a boyfriend on the side is OK if I have priority." These data, when compared with normative lesbian sexual monogamy in lover relationships (although casual, promiscuous lesbian encounters in between lovers are not uncommon), tend to reinforce a widely held view that males are promiscuous whereas females are not (cf. Symons, 1979, chapter 9). This, in turn, leads to the conjecture that a male/male lover relationship is likely to survive only if nonexclusive, the opposite tending to be true for lesbians.

One would expect, therefore, to find several significantly different patterns of sexually nonexclusive male/male lover relationships. These would include couples who are officially committed to a monogamistic ideal and whose outside sexual activities are done on the sly; couples breaking up in response to the discovery of infidelities; couples originally committed to monogamy who have discovered lapses and are in the process of redefining the ground rules; stable couples with comfortable, openly nonexclusive ground rules; and long-standing lover couples who are no longer sexually involved with each other but who still sleep together (cf. Douglas, 1973).

There is good reason to expect significant correlations between these patterns and the important dimensions we have already identified as missing from the Bell and Weinberg study. First, consider acculturation. The dominant heterosexual cultural ideal is a monogamistic lover relationship or "marriage." In contrast, the male gay subculture puts a premium on casual, recreational sex and tends to view monogamy as an aberration. Thus, one's desire for monogamy or nonexclusivity in a male homosexual lover relationship can be expected to correlate in a statistically significant manner with the degree of one's acculturation to the male gay subculture. It is plausible to assume that male/male couples who insist on monogamy are alienated from both the dominant heterosexual culture and the male homosexual subculture. In light of the comments about subculture acculturation and autonomy of self-worth made previously, it would appear that in most male/male couples of considerable duration partners who insist on monogamy would prove less well-adjusted psychologically than those in comfortably and openly nonexclusive stable relationships.

Second, although very few empirical studies have been done on the connections between jealousy, sexual nonexclusivity, and "power-plays" within lover or couple relationships, what little work there is suggests that the success of a sexually nonexclusive relationship depends on the extent to which partners are equally committed to the relationship and on the degree of autonomy of self-worth enjoyed by both partners (White, Note 6; Walster, Traupmann, & Walster, 1978; see also Clanton & Smith, 1977). The marked propensity of males to be promiscuous (Symons, 1979, chapter 9), reinforced by male gay subcultural pressures toward promiscuity, makes long-term, sexually exclusive, male/male lover relationships highly unlikely. The ways in which sexual nonexclusivity is dealt with so that jealousy does not consume the relationship can be expected to be an important correlate of psychological adjustment.

In my opinion, the two points just raised tap crucial dimensions of male/male lover relationships, dimensions strongly affecting the success and survival of the relationships and totally absent from the data used to generate the Bell and Weinberg typology of homosexualities. This lack renders suspect the "naturalness" or "genuineness" of their division of "open" and "closed coupleds." While the nomenclature for these classifications suggests that the open- and closed-coupled taxa distinction is based on adherence to, or violation of, canons of sexual exclusivity or monogamy, this is a fundamental misperception. Bell (Note 2) stresses that monogamy is not the basis of the open- vs. closed-coupled dichotomy; rather, with respect to the "number of sexual partners" parameters, it is a statistically relative distinction. Thus, participants in both open- and closed-coupled partnerships may be nonmonogamous, the relative frequencies of extrarelational sexual contacts being the key differentiating factor in the assignment to the two taxa. (Recall that approximately 25% of their sample were nonassignable to any taxon.)

These caveats aside, the diagnostic criteria are defective. Specifically, they force heterogeneous collections into unnatural taxa. The "closed coupled" taxon lumps together the following groups: monogamous couples, nonexclusive couples who have occasional outside encounters (openly or covertly), highly nonexclusive couples who confine their "extramarital" activity to secondary lovers or a small stable of regulars, etc. Similarly, the "open-coupled" taxon lumps together couples whose relationships are threatened by extensive covert "extramarital" activity, relationships in the process of collapsing under the pressure of unresolved "infidelities," and many highly stable and rewarding lover relationships where one or both partners engages in high-volume promiscuous sex. Thus, there is good reason to think that Bell's and Weinberg's "open coupled" and "closed coupled" taxa are highly artificial groupings which amalgamate different coupling patterns in ways that obfuscate the psychologically and sociologically significant differences. This casts doubt on Bell's and Weinberg's subsequent attempts to correlate taxon membership with other psychological and sociological dimensions.

It may be that further analysis and reduction of their raw data will confirm or refute these charges, and I encourage them to do such an analysis. However, because Bell's and Weinberg's interview schedule largely ignores dimensions of acculturation, psychological adjustment, and patterns of success or failure for male/male relationships, their data base is surely inadequate to establish whether my charges against their typology are correct or refutable. My best guess is that had they included in their schedule questions dealing with acculturation and lover-relationship management variables, Bell and Weinberg would have obtained a substantially different typology.

Conclusion

I fear it may seem to many readers that I have been trying to "do a job" on the Bell and Weinberg study and that my earlier comments in support of the substantial value of their study are polite but empty rhetoric. This is not the case. Given the sorry state of research on homosexuality, it is terribly important that the contradictory and conflicting claims of the literature be put to severe and large-sample empirical testing. The various shortcomings in Bell's and Weinberg's study do not seriously undercut the effectiveness of their effort in this direction. This is especially true by virtue of the fact that they employ a conceptual investigative apparatus that reflects and incorporates the range of variables employed in previous studies of homosexuality. To be sure, their efforts at a positive advancement of our understanding of homosexuality are less successful—largely because their choice of variables does not go significantly beyond those found in the earlier literature on homosexuality. Even so, what they have been able to find using an improved version of the traditional apparatus is a sizeable improvement over prior work. For example, using this apparatus they have dispelled many myths about the alleged psychological maladjustment of homosexual men and women—even if they have not fully fathomed the relevant dimensions of the psychological adjustments of participants in various homosexualities. Again I stress that it is precisely *because* of the merits of their study that my commentary here has been able to display significant unexplored dimensions of homosexual experiences.

The significance of the study's contribution to the literature on lesbianism should also be emphasized. Lester (1975) devotes a brief separate chapter (chapter 14) to a discussion of "female homosexuality" and surveys only 23 works, a number of which are only partially concerned with female homosexuality. By contrast, Bell's and Weinberg's study, which devotes approximately equal attention to female and male homosexuality, is clearly the single most significant piece of research on lesbianism to date. This said, I repeat my earlier comments about the need for significant acculturated lesbian input into research on female homosexuality.

Solid empirical research on homosexuality is neither impossible nor improbable. Indeed, I anticipate such research and expect that it will provide important insights into homosexuality and will improve on the impressive strides already achieved by Bell and Weinberg toward enlarging our understanding of homosexuality and sexuality in general.

FOOTNOTES

1. I confine my attention to the first volume, which focuses primarily "...upon diversity—the ways in which homosexuals differ from each other" (Bell & Weinberg, 1978, p. 25). These diversities include sexual circumstances, social lives, and psychological adjustment. The second volume (Bell, Weinberg, & Hammersmith, Note 1) makes "an attempt to ascertain the kinds of developmental experiences which are apt to lead to homosexuality or heterosexuality in men and women" (and thereby to test the main etiological theories).

2. Facile dismissals of statistical studies such as Bell's and Weinberg's maintain that their samples are not representative (i.e., do not reflect the total population with respect to demographic variables). An equally facile dismissal of such charges is to include caveats to the effect that the study is not intended to be representative of anything more than the sample population. While both tacks are legitimate at times, they tend to obfuscate important methodological issues surrounding sample representativeness. If the focus of a study is demographic, sample representativeness is crucial to the adequacy of the study. If the purpose is to explore diversity, sample representativeness is not particularly relevant, provided the sample is sufficiently diverse to represent the main variations in the parent population. On the other hand, if the focus of a study is on refuting general claims about a population, highly nonrepresentative samples from a biased subpopulation are adequate, although they cannot serve to establish general theses about the total population, let alone demographic profiles. When these subtleties are taken into account, criticisms that Bell's and Weinberg's sample is unrepresentative or dated are substantially defused.

3. In this respect it is worth noting the recent widespread employment of the "hanky code" among homosexual males when cruising to advertise sexual preferences. The color and location of bandannas are significant. When worn in the left pocket, the bandanna indicates a preference for the "active" or "aggressor" role and in the right rear pocket a preference for the "passive" or "recipient" role. In one popular code, dark-blue color indicates a preference for anal intercourse, light blue for fellatio, white for masturbation (mutual or self), black for heavy SM and whipping, gray for bondage, red for "fist-fucking," yellow for "water sports," brown for "scat games," olive drab for "uniform fetishes," purple for piercing scenes, orange for either "anything any time" or "nothing right now," etc. The incompleteness of this code should be noted. It excludes activities, such as analingus and "ball sucking," which are far more prevalent than many covered by the code, to say nothing of more esoteric acts such as "felching." A variant, lesbian code has recently been published (Samois, 1979, p. 79).

4. One should compare the claim with Table 7 (p. 310) where 63% of the homosexual re-

spondents told half or less of their tricks a fair amount about themselves, and 48% were told a fair amount about their tricks. (The discrepancy here makes the data suspect, incidentally.) The fact that 63% of the whites and 70% of blacks reported that more than half of their tricks were willing to give their addresses or phone numbers does not lend support to Bell's and Weinberg's conclusion. For two homosexual men to trade phone numbers is a fairly common, symbolic way of saying, "Thanks, it was good" and reveals nothing about how friendly the two become. More significant would have been figures on how many were willing to give their correct last name. It should also be noted that the tricks involved range from quickies in restrooms, steam baths, and "in the bushes" to people brought home; cf. note 6 below.

5. It should be noted that Hunt's sampling procedures are seriously defective in ways that tend to bias findings in favor of the sexually more liberated.

6. For conjectures in explanation of Masters' and Johnson's data that homosexual "lover" couples are so nonorgasmicentric, whereas assigned homosexual couples are orgasmicentric in a fashion similar to their heterosexual subjects, see Suppe (Note 3).

7. The most relevant questions on the interview schedule are:

377. Techniques used, reactions to them, and age of first and most recent use.
378. Frequency of use of various techniques in the last year.
379, 380. Proportion of time failed to reach orgasm during sex.

8. Sisley and Harris (1977) seems to me decidedly inferior to Silverstein and White (1977) and Fisher (1972) since it attempts to impose a normative conception of "a proper lesbian lifestyle," whereas the other two volumes accept as legitimate an impressive diversity of male homosexual life-styles; Califia (1980) provides a worthy antidote. Such works provide still another compromise surrogate for homosexual input into research-study design. These sources have, however, only become available since Bell and Weinberg mounted their study, so the authors cannot be faulted for not consulting the books. (Such sources as *The Beginners Guide to Cruising,* Guild Press, n.d., and the sequel, *The Advanced Guide,* were available then, however.)

9. A marvelous discussion of self-alienation is found in Book V, Chap. 5 ("The Grand Inquisitor") of Dostoevsky's *The Brothers Karamazov* (1937). A beautifully sensitive philosophical discussion of selfhood, alienation, freedom, etc. is found in Bergmann's *On Being Free* (1977). Note that homosexual persons who mask their sexual orientation from themselves also experience self-alienation.

10. Cf. Tables 13.1 and 13.3 of *Homosexualities.* For simplicity, and because the situation is more exaggerated, I am reporting the male data; in the lesbian data (Table 13.2) the correlations are somewhat different, none exceeding a correlation coefficient of 29, which is reflected in the loadings in Table 13.4.

11. My sample is almost certainly nonrepresentative, but in conversation with Pepper Schwartz about preliminary data from her "couples study," it appears that the pattern I have found is quite typical. Dr. Schwartz, however, has encountered a small but not inconsequential number of monogamistic exceptions of considerable duration.

REFERENCE NOTES

1. Bell, A. P., Weinberg, M., & Hammersmith, S. K. *Sexual preference: Its development among men and women.* Book in preparation.

2. Bell, A. P. *Homosexualities:* Comments and replies to criticisms. In N. Koertge (Chair), *Paradigms and prejudices in research on homosexuality.* Symposium presented at the meeting of the American Association for the Advancement of Science, Houston, 1979.

3. Suppe, F. *Homosexuality and Masters and Johnson's research program.* Manuscript submitted for publication, 1980.

4. Suppe, F. The Bell/Weinberg study and future priorities for research on homosexuality. In N. Koertge (Chair), *Paradigms and prejudices in research on homosexuality.* Symposium presented at the meeting of the American Association for the Advancement of Science, Houston, 1979.

5. Suppe, F. Theoretical perspectives on closure. In H. T. Englehardt, Jr., A. Kaplan, & D. Callahan (Eds.), *Values and politics in scientific debates: The resolution of controversy.* New York: Plenum Press, forthcoming.

6. White, G. L. *Inequality of emotional involvement, power, and jealousy in romantic couples.* Paper presented at the 85th Annual Convention of the American Psychological Association, San Francisco, August 1977.

REFERENCES

Bell, A. P. Research on homosexuality: Back to the drawing board. *Archives of Sexual Behavior,* 1975, *4,* 421-431.

Bell, A. P., & Weinberg, M. S. *Homosexualities: A study of diversity among men and women.* New York: Simon and Schuster, 1978.

Bergmann, F. *On being free.* South Bend, IN: University of Notre Dame Press, 1977.

Bieber, I., Dain, H. J., Dince, P. R., Drellich, M. G., Grand, H. G., Gundlach, R. H., Kremer, M. W., Rifkin, A. H., Wilber, C. B., & Bieber, T. *Homosexuality.* New York: Basic Books, 1962.

Blumstein, P. W., & Schwartz, P. Bisexuality: Some social psychological issues. *Journal of Social Issues,* 1977, *33,* 30-45.

Braaten, L., & Darling, C. Overt and covert homosexual problems among male college students. *Genetic Psychological Monographs,* 1965, *71,* 269-310.

Bradburn, N. M., & Caplovitz, C. *Reports on happiness.* Chicago: Aldine Publishing Co., 1965.

Broverman, I., Broverman, D. M., Clarkson, F. E., Rosenkranz, P. S., & Vogel, S. R. Sex role stereotypes and clinical judgments of mental health. *Journal of Consulting and Clinical Psychology,* 1970, *34,* 1-7.

Califia, P. *Sapphistry: The book of lesbian sexuality.* Tallahassee: Naiad Press, 1980.

Clanton, E. G., & Smith, L. G. *Jealousy.* Englewood Cliffs, NJ: Prentice Hall, 1977.

Cronbach, L. J. *Essentials of psychological testing* (2nd ed.). New York: Harper and Row, 1960.

Cubitt, C., & Gendreau, P. Assessing the diagnostic utility of MMPI and 16PF indices of homosexuality in a prison sample. *Journal of Consulting and Clinical Psychology,* 1972, *39,* 342.

Dahlstrom, W. G., Welsh, G. S., & Dahlstrom, L. E. *An MMPI handbook* (Rev. ed., Vol. 1). Minneapolis: University of Minnesota Press, 1972.

Dean, R. B., & Richardson, H. Analysis of MMPI profiles of 40 college-educated overt male homosexuals. *Journal of Consulting Psychology,* 1964, *28,* 483-486.

Deutsch, H. Homosexuality in women. In J. Marmor (Ed.), *Sexual inversion,* New York: Basic Books, 1965.

Dewhurst, K. Sexual activity and urinary steroids in man with special reference to homosexuality. *British Journal of Psychiatry,* 1969, *115,* 1413-1415.

Doidge, W., & Holtzman, W. Implications of homosexuality among Air Force trainees. *Journal of Consulting Psychology,* 1960, *24,* 9-13.

Dostoevsky, F. *The brothers Karamazov.* New York: Modern Library, 1937.

Douglas, A. *Friends: A true story of male love.* New York: Coward, McCann, Geogheagan, 1973.

Ellis, A., & Abarbanal, A. (Eds.). *The encyclopedia of sexual behavior.* New York: Hawthorn Books, 1967.

Fisher, P. *The gay mystique.* New York: Stein and Day, 1972.

Freedman, M. *Homosexuality and psychological functioning.* Belmont, CA: Brooks/Cole, 1971.

Fromm, E. O., & Elonen, A. S. The use of projective techniques in the study of a case of female homosexuality. *Journal of Projective Techniques,* 1951, *15,* 185-230.

Giannell, A. S. Giannell's criminosynthesis theory applied to female homosexuality. *Journal of Psychology,* 1966, *64,* 213-232.

Ginsburg, K. N. The "meat rack": A study of the male homosexual prostitute. *American*

Journal of Psychotherapy, 1967, *21,* 171-185.

Gonsiorek, J. G. Psychological adjustment and homosexuality. JSAS *Catalog of Selected Documents in Psychology,* 1977, *7,* 45. (Ms. No. 1478)

Goodstein, L. D. Regional differences in MMPI responses among male college students. *Journal of Consulting Psychology,* 1954, *18,* 437-441.

Graham, J., Schroeder, H. E., & Lilly, R. S. Factor analysis of items on the social introversion and masculinity-femininity scales of the MMPI. *Journal of Clinical Psychology,* 1971, *27,* 367-370.

Hathaway, Sr. R., & McKinley, J. C. *The MMPI manual* (Rev. ed.). New York: The Psychological Corp., 1967.

Henry, G. W., & Galbraith, H. M. Constitutional factors in homosexuals. *American Journal of Psychiatry,* 1964, *8,* 157-159.

Hoenig, J., & Torr, J. B. D. Karo-typing of a transsexualist. *Journal of Psychosomatic Research,* 1964, *8,* 157-159.

Hoffman, M. *The gay world.* New York: Basic Books, 1968.

Humphreys, L. *Tearoom trade: Impersonal sex in public places.* Chicago: Aldine, 1970.

Hunt, M. *Sexual behavior in the 1970s.* Chicago: Playboy Press, 1974.

Institute for Sex Research. *A study of socialization—1969-1970.* Unpublished confidential document, 1969-1970.

Kaye, H., Berl, S., Clare, J., Eleston, M. R., Gershwin, B. S., Gershwin, P., Kogan, L. S., Torda, C., & Wilber, C. B. Homosexuality in women. *Archive of General Psychiatry,* 1967, *17,* 626-634.

Keiser, S., & Schaffer, D. Environmental factors in homosexuality in adolescent girls. *Psychoanalytic Review,* 1949, *36,* 283-295.

Kinsey, A. C., Pomeroy, W., & Martin, C. *Sexual behavior in the human male.* Philadelphia: Saunders, 1948.

Lang, T. Studies in the genetic determinants of homosexuality. *Journal of Nervous and Mental Disease,* 1949, *92,* 55-64.

Lee, J. A. Going public: A study in the sociology of homosexual liberation. *Journal of Homosexuality* 1977, *3* (1), 49-78.

Lester, D. *Unusual sexual behavior: The standard deviations.* Springfield, IL: Charles C. Taylor, 1975.

Levine, M. P. The sociology of male homosexuality and lesbianism: An introductory bibliography. *Journal of Homosexuality,* 1980, *5* (3), 249-275.

Loraine, J. A., Ismail, A. A. A., Adamopoulos, D. A., & Dove, G. A. Endocrine functions in male and female homosexuals. *British Medical Journal,* 1970, *4,* 406-408.

Manosevitz, M. Education and MMPI Mf scores in homosexual and heterosexual males. *Journal of Consulting and Clinical Psychology,* 1971, *36,* 395-399.

Margolese, M. S. Homosexuality: A new endocrine correlate. *Hormones and Behavior,* 1970, *1,* 151-155.

Masters, R., & Johnson, V. *Homosexuality in perspective.* Boston: Little, Brown, 1979.

Morin, S. F. An annotated bibliography of research on lesbianism and male homosexuality (1967-1977). In JSAS *Catalog of Selected Documents in Psychology,* 1976, *6,* 15. (Ms. No. 1191)

Oliver, W. A., & Mosher, D. L. Psychopathology and guilt in heterosexual and subgroups of homosexual reformatory inmates. *Journal of Abnormal Psychology,* 1968, *73,* 323-329.

Quine, W. V. *Word and object.* New York: Technology Press and John Wiley, 1960.

Rechy, J. *City of night.* New York: Grove Press, 1963.

Rogers, C. *On becoming a person.* Boston: Houghton Mifflin, 1961.

Rogers, C. *Becoming partners: Marriage and its alternatives.* New York: Dell, 1972.

Rosenberg, M. *Society and the adolescent self-image.* Princeton, NJ: Princeton University Press, 1965.

Rubins, J. The neurotic personality and certain sexual perversions. *Contemporary Psychoanalysis,* 1968, *14,* 53-72.

Ruse, M. Are there gay genes? Sociobiology and homosexuality. *Journal of Homosexuality,* 1981, *6*(4), 5-34.

Samois. Things that go bump in the night. *Drummer: America's Mag for the Macho Man,* 1979, No. 31, p. 79.

Shively, M. G., & De Cecco, J. Components of sexual identity. *Journal of Homosexuality,* 1977, *3*(1), 41-48.

Silverstein, C., & White, E. *The joy of gay sex.* New York: Crown Publishers, 1977.

Sisley, E. L., & Harris, B. *The joy of lesbian sex.* New York: Crown Publishers, 1977.

Socarides, C. W. *The overt homosexual.* New York: Grune and Stratton, 1968.

Sokal, R., & Sneath, J. *Principles of numerical taxonomy.* San Francisco: W. H. Freeman and Co., 1963.

Stace, W. T. *Mysticism and philosophy.* Philadelphia: Lippincott, 1960.

Suppe, F. Some philosophical problems in biological speciation and taxonomy. In J. Wojcie-chowski (Ed.), *Conceptual basis of the classification of knowledge.* Munich: Verlag Dokumentation, 1974.

Suppe, F. (Ed.). *The structure of scientific theories* (2nd ed.). Urbana, IL: University of Illinois Press, 1977.

Symons, D. *The evolution of human sexuality.* New York: Oxford University Press, 1979.

Townsend, L. *The leatherman's handbook.* San Francisco: Le Salon, 1972.

Tripp, C. A. *The homosexual matrix.* New York: McGraw-Hill, 1975.

Veldman, D. J. *Fortran programming for the behavioral sciences.* New York: Holt, Rinehart, and Winston, 1967.

Walster, E., Traupmann, J., & Walster, G. W. Equity and extramarital sexuality. *Archives of Sexual Behavior,* 1978, *7*, 127-142.

Ward, J. H. Hierarchical grouping to optimize an objective function. *American Statistical Association Journal,* 1963, *58*, 236-244.

Weinberg, M. S., & Bell, A. P. (Eds.). *Homosexuality: An annotated bibliography.* New York: Harper and Row, 1972.

Weinberg, M. S., & Williams, C. J. *Male homosexuals: Their problems and adaptations.* New York: Oxford University Press, 1974.

Weinberg, M. S., & Williams, C. J. Gay baths and their social organization of impersonal sex. *Social Problems,* 1975, *23*, 124-136.

NOTES ON THE CONTRIBUTORS

—Lynda I. A. Birke, PhD, studied animal behavior at Sussex University and worked in the History and Social Studies of Science Department there. She is now a Research Fellow in Biology at the Open University in Milton Keynes. She is co-author of *Alice Through the Microscope: The Power of Science Over Women's Lives* and has recently published a book on menstruation.

—John P. De Cecco, PhD, director of the Center for Homosexual Education, Evaluation and Research, will already be known to readers through his numerous scientific publications and as editor of this journal. He is Professor of Psychology and teaches in the Human Sexuality Program at San Francisco State University.

—Noretta Koertge, PhD, studied history and philosophy of science at the University of London and now teaches in that department at Indiana University. She has written numerous articles on both historical and contemporary theories of scientific method. A novel, *Who Was That Masked Woman?*, which describes a lesbian's search for identity, is forthcoming from St. Martin's Press. She is the guest editor of this special issue.

—Michael Ruse, PhD, studied philosophy of science at Bristol University and now teaches in Canada at Guelph University. His books include *The Philosophy of Biology, The Darwinian Revolution,* and *Sociobiology: Sense or Nonsense?* Forthcoming from the University of California Press is *Homosexuality: A Philosophical Perspective.*

—Frederick Suppe, PhD, studied philosophy and computer science at Michigan and is now Chairperson of History and Philosophy of Science at the University of Maryland, where he teaches a very well-received, clinically oriented philosophy course on human sexuality. His book, *The Structure of Scientific Theories,* is now in its second edition. A current research interest is methodological issues in research on homosexuality. He is a consulting editor of this journal.

Journal of Homosexuality, Vol. 6(4), Summer 1981

INDEX TO VOLUME 6

Articles (Issue No.) **Page**

Birke, L. I. A. *Is Homosexuality Hormonally Determined?* (4) 35
Burg, B. R. *Ho Hum, Another Work of the Devil: Buggery and Sodomy in Early Stuart England.* (1/2) 69

Cochran, S. D. *See* Peplau, L. A. (3) 1
Crompton, L. *The Myth of Lesbian Impunity: Capital Laws from 1270-1791.* (1/2) 11

Davison, G. C. *Sexual Orientation Stereotypy in the Distortion of Clinical Judgment.* (3) 37
De Cecco, J. P. *Definition and Meaning of Sexual Orientation.* (4) 51
Duberman, M. B. *"Writhing Bedfellows": 1826-Two Young Men from Antebellum South Carolina's Ruling Elite Share "Extravagant Delight."* (1/2) 85

Eriksson, B. *A Lesbian Execution in Germany, 1721: The Trial Records.* (1/2) 27

Friedman, S. *See* Davison, G. C. (3) 37

Gilbert, A. N. *Conceptions of Homosexuality and Sodomy in Western History.* (1/2) 57

Haeberle, E. J. *"Stigmata of Degeneration": Prisoner Markings in Nazi Concentration Camps.* (1/2) 35

Kennedy, H. C. *The "Third Sex" Theory of Karl Heinrich Ulrichs.* (1/2) 103

Lautmann, R. *The Pink Triangle: The Persecution of Homosexual Males in Concentration Camps in Nazi Germany.* (1/2) 141
Licata, S. J. *The Homosexual Rights Movement in the United States: A Traditionally Overlooked Area of American History.* (1/2) 161
Lucas, J. *See* Wise, T. N. (3) 61

MacDonald Jr., A. P. *Bisexuality: Some Comments on Research and Theory.* (3) 21
McDonald, G. *Misrepresentation, Liberalism, and Heterosexual Bias in Introductory Psychology Textbooks.* (3) 45
Monter, E. W. *Sodomy and Heresy in Early Modern Switzerland.* (1/2) 41

Navin, H. *Medical and Surgical Risks in Handballing: Implications of an Inadequate Socialization Process.* (3) 67

Oaks, R. F. *Defining Sodomy in Seventeenth-Century Massachusetts.* (1/2) 79

Parker, W. *Homosexuality in History: An Annotated Bibliography.* (1/2) 191
Peplau, L. A. *Value Orientations in the Intimate Relationships of Gay Men.* (3) 1

Journal of Homosexuality, Vol. 6(4), Summer 1981

Ruse, M. *Are There Gay Genes? Sociobiology and Homosexuality.* (4) 5

Suppe, F. *The Bell and Weinberg Study: Future Priorities for Research on
Homosexuality.* (4) 69

Weeks, J. *Inverts, Perverts, and Mary-Annes: Male Prostitution and the Regulation of
Homosexuality in England in the Nineteenth and Early Twentieth Centuries.* (1/2) 113
Wise, T. N. *Pseudotranssexualism: Iatrogenic Gender Dysphoria.* (3) 61

Book Reviews
Bonds, W. N. *The Unmentionable Vice: Homosexuality in the Later Medieval Period,*
by Michael Goodrich. (1/2) 212
Bullough, V. L. *The Unmentionable Vice: Homosexuality in the Later Medieval Period,*
by Michael Goodich. (1/2) 211

Goldstein, B. *Sexual Excitement/Sexual Peace,* by Suzanne Sarnoff and Irving Sarnoff. (3) 95
Gonsiorek, J. C. *Homosexuality in Perspective,* by William H. Masters and
Virginia E. Johnson. (3) 81

Kessler, D. R. *Homosexuality,* by Charles W. Socarides. (3) 89

Ostrow, D. G. *Sexually Transmitted Diseases: Guide to Diagnosis and Therapy,* by
Robert C. Noble, and *Venerelogy in Practice: The Sexually Committed Diseases,*
by Neils Hjorth and Henning Schmidt. (3) 100

Smith, R. W. *Masculinity and Femininity: Their Psychological Dimensions, Correlates
and Antecedents,* by Janet T. Spence and Robert L. Helmreich. (3) 77

Weinrich, J. D. *Sex, Hormones and Behaviour,* Ciba Foundation Symposium 62. (3) 104

DATE DUE